Rosemary Watt-W

RUSSIAN REVOLUTION

UNIFORM WITH THIS BOOK

RICHARD PROCKTOR *Nazi Germany*

IN PREPARATION

LOIS MITCHISON *Red China*

A BODLEY HEAD CONTEMPORARY HISTORY

RUSSIAN REVOLUTION

RONALD HINGLEY

THE BODLEY HEAD
LONDON   SYDNEY
TORONTO

ISBN 0 370 01560 6

© Ronald Hingley 1970
Maps © The Bodley Head Ltd 1970
Printed and bound in Great Britain for
The Bodley Head Ltd
9 Bow Street, London WC2
by William Clowes & Sons, Beccles.
Set in Monophoto Baskerville
First published 1970

CONTENTS

ACKNOWLEDGMENTS

For their kindness in reading and commenting on my manuscript I am greatly indebted to my wife, and to three colleagues: Professor Michael Futrell, Dr H. Shukman and Mr H. T. Willetts.

Thanks are due to the following for permission to use copyright photographs:

Hulton Picture Library, pages 12/13, 19, 24, 27, 30, 40, 45, 46, 50, 52, 54, 62, 72, 81, 87, 91, 96, 99, 104, 112, 116, 119, 121; Staatsbibliotek, Berlin, pages 10, 17, 29, 44, 47, 74, 107; Novosti Press Agency, pages 14, 18, 32, 35, 59, 60, 69, 76, 88; Camera Press Ltd., pages 37, 66, 110, 115; The Imperial War Museum, pages 93, 109; Culver Pictures, New York, page 43; The Mansell Collection, page 23.

1

Russia:
the Country and
its Peoples

The revolutions of 1917 brought great changes to the old Russian Empire, including a new kind of government and a new name—the Soviet Union. But the country is still commonly referred to as Russia, and some of its features have remained unchanged since 1917.

It is still the largest country in the world, the next being Canada, which is not even half as extensive. From its western frontiers to Vladivostok in the east Russia stretches about six thousand miles, and it measures about three thousand miles from north to south at its widest point. It has a large population, numbering about 230 million in the 1960s—an increase of about 100 million since the beginning of the century. The country is not overcrowded, however, for there are still vast areas where no one lives at all. China and India have far larger populations living on smaller territories.

The largest part of Russia lies in Asia, and includes Siberia, which is as big as the lighted portion of the full moon. But the most important part is European Russia, where the majority of the population lives and where many of the country's main historical events have occurred.

Much of European Russia is flat—a great plain extending beyond the comparatively low Ural Mountains (which separate European from Asian Russia) far into Siberia. The far north of the country consists of arctic

THE SOVI

O C E A N

Khatanga

Bulun

Lena

E R I A

Arctic Circle

Yakutsk

Lena

KAMCHATKA

Magadan

SEA OF
OKHOTSK

SAKHALIN

P A C I F I C   O C E A N

Angara

Irkutsk

Lake Baikal

Amur

M O N G O L I A

Vladivostok

SEA OF
JAPAN

J A P A N

H   I   N   A

KOREA

Peking

YELLOW
SEA

EDGAR HOLLOWAY

0   500   1000 MILES

0   500   1000 K M

wastes and frozen swamp (tundra). South of this there is a belt of forest, then one of grassland (steppe), and then one of desert. Ranges of very high mountains, the Caucasus and others, fence off large parts of southern and far eastern Russia. Huge rivers flow through the land, and are so wide in places that it is impossible to see from one bank to the other. They freeze in winter, as do some of the seas, with the result that many Russian ports need icebreakers to keep them open all the year round.

To lose one's way in the cruel blizzards of a Russian winter is to risk freezing to death. Siberia is even colder than European Russia, and the frozen wastes of the far north can barely support life. In summer, however, some of the coldest parts can be very hot, and Siberia itself has heat-waves and mosquitoes.

Before the days of trains, cars and aircraft it was especially hard to move from one part of Russia to another since travelling conditions were so primitive. Deep, sticky mud choked the mostly unpaved roads in spring and autumn, cutting off many villages for weeks on end. Even when conditions were ideal, sheer distance made journeying a lengthy process, whether by river boat, carriage or the open sledges on which travellers crossed the winter snows after wrapping themselves in thick furs and sheepskins. They would press on through the night as well as by day—partly because the coaching stations were so draughty, noisy and infested with insects that no one would linger for a moment longer than was necessary to change horses. Travelling round the clock, the Emperor's couriers could average two hundred miles in twenty-four hours in the best conditions—that is, using sledges over hard snow. In this way it was possible to go from St Petersburg to Irkutsk in Siberia in as little as nineteen days, but such a journey might take far longer under worse conditions. Fortunately Russians have never seemed to be as concerned about time as many other peoples.

Although the country is called Russia, by no means all its citizens are Russians. The population is amazingly varied, and was so in the days of the Empire. For instance, the census of 1897 showed that only about 56 million out of 126 million—less than half the people of the Empire— were Russians. Two other large groups were Ukrainians and Belorussians —who are, like the Russians, members of the eastern branch of the Slav peoples. In the nineteenth century Poland and Finland both formed part of the Russian Empire, while the most numerous of the other peoples included Tatars, Germans, Jews, Georgians, Armenians, Estonians, Latvians and Lithuanians.

◄ The Nevsky Prospekt in St Petersburg, 1884.

Moscow and the Kremlin in the mid-nineteenth century. A contemporary painting

The peoples of the Empire spoke well over a hundred different languages, and they practised many different kinds of religion, including Moslem as well as Christian varieties. The most important religious denomination was the Russian Orthodox Church, the branch of eastern Christianity to which Russians, Ukrainians and Belorussians mostly belonged.

Religious practices are discouraged or forbidden by the Soviet Government which has ruled Russia since 1917, but in Imperial times many Russians thought that being Orthodox was the same thing as being Russian —it was natural to any patriot. The Orthodox Church had an even stronger hold on the villages than it had on the towns, and its complicated calendar gave a special shape and meaning to the peasants' lives. They frequently crossed themselves, they hung icons, or holy pictures, in their huts, and they kept the many strict fasts during which they were not allowed to consume milk or meat. But there were also many church

12

festivals and saints' days when the Orthodox indulged in drunken orgies—often the village priest as much as anyone.

By far the largest part of the population—four out of every five citizens—were peasants, and it may therefore be helpful to think of Imperial Russia as a great collection of scattered villages dotted over a vast expanse of territory with their huts of logs or clay and their wide, unpaved roads which were generally a mass of churned mud, dust or snow.

Two great cities have played an outstandingly important role in Russian history. These are Moscow, the present-day capital, situated in the heart of European Russia, and Leningrad in the north-west near the mouth of the River Neva. Under its original name of St Petersburg (1703 to 1914) and then of Petrograd (1914 to 1924), this was the capital of Russia between 1712 and 1918. Petrograd became the main scene of the 1917 revolutions, and many other important revolutionary events also took place there.

Besides being the seat of government in Imperial times, St Petersburg was also the centre for the court of the Russian Emperors, or Tsars, with its elaborate ceremonies including religious services and numerous court balls. The crowds on the Nevsky Prospekt, the city's most fashionable boulevard, included many generals and guards officers, besides hosts of civil servants who also wore uniform. Most St Petersburgers seemed to be on parade when they appeared in public, and to some the city seemed like one huge barracks. But it was also a highly cosmopolitan capital with its many foreign embassies and large foreign population. As a port it had easy communication with western Europe, and most St Petersburgers prided themselves on being up-to-date and in close touch with the modern world.

Moscow presented an entirely different picture. After losing its position as the capital of Russia in 1712, it remained old-fashioned and easy-going. In many ways the city was like yet another huge, sprawling village, but one full of churches with onion domes and the sound of bells. The unfashionable clothes worn by Muscovites, and even the cut of their whiskers, made St Petersburgers smile. Muscovites, however, thought of themselves as the real Russians, and it was in their old citadel, the Kremlin, that the Tsars were always crowned.

A typical Russian village at the turn of the century

2

Russia
before 1800

Imperial Russia was in many ways backward, undeveloped and quaint by
comparison with the more advanced societies of western Europe such as
England, France and Germany. When visitors from these countries came
to Moscow before the time of Peter the Great, who reigned from 1682 to
1725, they were deafened by the frequent ringing of church bells and
astonished by outlandish clothes and manners. The Russians were admittedly Christians, if of an unfamiliar kind, but they kept their women in
seclusion. Their style of dress also made them seem oriental and alien, as
did such habits as kowtowing—banging the head on the ground to show
respect for a superior. They flogged, tortured and executed criminals in
public, and left corpses dangling on the gallows for months as an example
to others—practices such as were admittedly not unknown at the time in
parts of the world considered more civilised.

Though Peter the Great by no means abandoned public executions, he
made an end of certain other native Russian customs among the upper
classes. He wanted above all to modernise the country, and therefore put
his gentlemen and officials into western European clothes such as he himself had taken to wearing in Moscow's German Quarter and when touring
western Europe. He would not let them kowtow, and he made them shave
off the beards which Russian men of all classes had worn up to this time.

The great Tsar even took scissors and snipped off their beards himself, and he sliced off the flowing sleeves of their traditional Russian robes. His aim was to make his officials and gentry look like modern western Europeans. In any case many of his civil servants actually were western Europeans since he hired foreigners to help him administer the country. However, Peter left Russian peasants, priests and merchants their beards and old-fashioned dress. He seemed to have created two different species of Russian, and the differences continued long after his death.

Despite Peter's efforts to modernise Russia, the country remained comparatively backward after his death, partly because of the very rift which he had created or widened between a europeanised gentry and a primitive peasantry. One notably barbarous feature of Russian society was serfdom, the system whereby estate-owners from the gentry possessed the people who tilled the land along with the land itself. These serfs—slaves in effect—were sometimes treated worse than domestic animals.

It was a miserable fate to find oneself in the tree-bark shoes of a bearded serf who lived in a beetle-ridden, crowded, smoky hut, and had little in the way of freedom, money, food or privilege. In the eighteenth century Catherine the Great gave serf-owners the right to punish their peasants with imprisonment and exile in Siberia, or by sending them into the army for twenty-five years. A master could split serf families—selling the children into slavery elsewhere, and keeping their parents. He could prevent his serfs from marrying, or he could make them marry against their will, breeding them like cattle. He could turn them into a ballet troupe, or have them flogged to death in his stables, and without anyone showing much surprise in either event.

The master also had numerous serfs to wait on him as his personal servants, sometimes responsible for such things as filling his tobacco-pipe and serving his claret at the proper temperature, while he—clean-shaven, politely spoken, perhaps talking better French than Russian—seemed to belong to a different order of being. Although some of the poorer and coarser gentlemen resembled their own serfs in their manner of life, on the whole gentlemen and peasants stood at opposite poles with no one of great importance in between. Admittedly there were also merchants, craftsmen and other townspeople, but these did not develop into a powerful middle class such as has played a large part in the history of other countries.

Lacking an effective middle class, Russia also lagged behind more advanced countries in the development of her industry and technology, though it is also true that the Urals led the world in the production of pig-iron in the late eighteenth century. In general Russia had more primitive machines, a lower level of general education and culture, poorer roads, worse famines and more serious epidemics than the chief countries of western Europe. Above all, her form of government seemed antiquated and oriental.

This system, autocracy, consisted of rule by a single person—the Autocrat, Emperor or Tsar—who was above any law and could behave exactly as he wished. A Tsar could send anyone, prince or serf, to exile in Siberia, imprison him, or have him beaten or killed. He might have favourites, high officials or—in the nineteenth century—ministers to help him govern, but he was under no obligation to take their advice and he could dismiss them at will.

Many European countries had once had emperors or kings possessing absolute power like that of the Tsars. However, these monarchs gradually lost power to others—for instance, to parliaments—with the result that wider circles of people began to exercise some measure of control. The

The interior of a peasant hut.

Barge-haulers, 1912

Russian Tsar by contrast, tended to gain power rather than lose it, the common people had no influence on government at all, and members of the upper classes only had as much as the Tsar allowed them.

The Tsar had a large number of officials, high and low, serving throughout the country to ensure that his orders were obeyed—orders which were often complicated and self-contradictory, or were delayed in transit. A local bureaucrat, especially the governor of a province, could therefore behave like a little Tsar within his own area—particularly if it was far away from the capital. Officials committed outrageous abuses and became notorious for bullying, obstructionism and using harsh laws to threaten people, and thus extort bribes.

The miserable conditions of the country caused despair and unrest among the peasants. Angry villagers would frequently riot against the local landowner, loot his house and burn it down—perhaps lynching him and his family. Soldiers would then be ordered to shoot and flog the rioters. Sometimes so many peasants took part that their riots turned into civil wars, and they fought pitched battles against armies sent by the government. Such were the peasant and Cossack revolts led by Stenka Razin in the seventeenth century and by Yemelyan Pugachov a century later. Pugachov pretended to be the real Tsar, and his followers killed many hundreds of landowners before he was betrayed to Catherine the Great's troops, taken to Moscow in a cage and beheaded. Dangerous as they were, however, these peasant revolts were not revolutions in the strict sense, since those who took part were chiefly concerned with robbery, revenge or adventure—not with changing the government.

In the eighteenth century the upper classes developed a style of revolt entirely different from that of the peasant rebellions—the so-called palace revolutions. But these were not true revolutions either, for the aim of such

The interior of Kara prison in Siberia in the late nineteenth century

conspirators was only to remove an individual ruler whom they disliked by substituting someone more congenial. This might present no great difficulties to a group of determined guardsmen in St Petersburg. They would set off at dead of night, break into the imperial palace, seize an Emperor and imprison or murder him—as happened to the baby Tsar Ivan VI in 1741, to Peter III in 1762 and to Paul I in 1801. It was by these means that the two most important eighteenth-century Empresses—Elizabeth and Catherine the Great—came to power, both as usurpers. The strangling of the Emperor Paul I in his palace by drunken guards officers in the small hours of 12 March 1801 was the last *coup d'état* of this kind, a palace revolution which brought his son Alexander I to the throne as the first of the nineteenth-century Tsars.

3

The Decembrist Revolt

It might have been expected that a Russian revolutionary movement, when it came, would be largely the work of downtrodden peasants rising against their oppressors. But though peasant revolutionaries were not unknown, it was educated people such as gentlemen and priests' sons who took the main initiative in preparing to overthrow the autocracy. This tendency was already evident in the late eighteenth century, when several writers, revolutionary in the sense that they published criticism of the government, emerged from the class of the gentry. One of these, Alexander Radishchev, gained fame as the 'first Russian radical', though he came no nearer to transforming society than publishing a scathing indictment of serfdom. For this he was sentenced to death, then reprieved and exiled to Siberia. His example helped to inspire the first real attempt at a Russian revolution —that provoked by the death of the Emperor Alexander I in 1825—in which officers of the guards were prominent.

The officers and gentlemen who attempted this *coup* in December 1825 later came to be called Decembrists. Many of them had served in western Europe during the Napoleonic wars of 1813–15, and had been impressed by the superiority of foreign forms of government. When the campaigns were over, they returned to Russia and began to form secret societies to plot the overthrow of the Tsar. Some Decembrists wished to abolish the monarchy altogether and set up a republic, while others planned to keep the Tsar, restricting his activities by a constitution laying down the exact limits of his power. Alexander I received information about these plots, but said that it was not for him to punish those concerned since he himself had held similar views as a young man.

When the news of Alexander's death reached St Petersburg on 27 November 1825, troops and officials began to follow the practice usual on the death of a Tsar by swearing loyalty to his heir. Alexander had left no son, which made Constantine, the eldest of his three surviving brothers, the successor in law. Such, at least, was the general impression, and it was to Constantine that the oath of loyalty was accordingly administered. In fact, however, Constantine had formally abandoned his claim to rule several years earlier. This meant that the real heir was a younger brother, the Grand Duke Nicholas, though even he was in some doubt about the true state of affairs since Constantine's renunciation of the crown had been kept a close secret. For two weeks Russia seemed to have no Tsar at all, or possibly two Tsars.

By the morning of 14 December the matter had at last been settled in favour of Nicholas and the troops received orders to swear loyalty to him— at the very time when the conspiring Decembrists happened to launch their attempted revolution in the form of a mutiny by military units stationed in the capital. Though members of many units did obey orders by taking the oath to Nicholas I, Decembrist junior officers in certain regiments had persuaded the common soldiers that the new Tsar was engaged in usurping the crown from Constantine, the rightful monarch.

They marched the men to the Senate Square—a large open place near the Tsar's Winter Palace—with the vague intention of persuading the Senate, a body of advisers to the Tsar, to declare the autocracy overthrown in favour of government by the mutineers. But the mutineers had no adequate plan of campaign, and some of their leaders did not even put in an appearance. For a time the rising seemed more like a peaceful demonstration than an attempt to seize power. The rebel troops began to cheer for Constantine and Constitution, believing that constitution was the name of Constantine's wife. It was too cold and windy to feel very enthusiastic even for such a romantic cause as this, however, and no one seemed to know what the next step should be.

The new Tsar, Nicholas I, was a ruthless man, but he did not wish to begin his reign by killing his subjects. For hours he tried unsuccessfully to

The executed Decembrist leaders

persuade the mutineers, of whom there were several thousand, to disperse peacefully. There were isolated acts of violence, including the shooting of Count Miloradovich, the Military Governor of St Petersburg, by one of the rebels. Then the Tsar ordered his cavalry to charge, but without effect since the horses were not properly shod and slipped on the icy cobbles.

Finally, as darkness fell, Nicholas ordered his artillery to fire on the mutineers. They fled, leaving dozens of dead and wounded behind them. Some ran over the frozen River Neva, where cannon balls broke the ice, and many people fell through and were drowned. That night loyal troops bivouacked by camp fires in the square, while the police hurriedly washed the blood off the cobbles and removed the dirty snow. They pushed the corpses under the ice of the river—and also, it was believed, some of the wounded.

The Tsar himself questioned the survivors. He staged a mass trial in secret, and hundreds received sentences of exile and imprisonment in Siberia. Five leaders were hanged on a bastion of the Peter and Paul Fortress in St Petersburg, and became famous as the first martyrs of Russian revolution.

The Decembrists inspired many later Russian revolutionaries, but more because they were pioneers who had died and suffered for their cause than because they had planned and fought for it effectively.

23

4

Nicholas I
and Alexander II

After beginning his reign by crushing a revolution, Nicholas I decided to ensure that there should never be another. He set up special police forces, the Third Section and the Gendarmes, to protect him against political plots. He also established a censorship to prevent anyone from criticising him in print, and he strictly controlled schools and universities to prevent ideas—about freedom or anything else—from reaching young people. They would do better to learn obedience, he thought, being an army officer by training, and one who sometimes spoke of the whole Empire as his military command.

In the Russian parts of the Empire, Nicholas kept revolution well in check. But there were some serious riots and army mutinies, and in 1830 revolution broke out in Poland, at this time part of the Russian Empire. It was a national rebellion against rule by Russia, and coincided with other revolutions in France and Belgium. After a large-scale military campaign, Nicholas's armies suppressed the Poles. The next alarm occurred in 1848–9, when revolution erupted once more in several European countries. Though it did not spread to Russia on this occasion, Nicholas was an enemy of all rebellion against authority even outside his empire, for which reason he came to be called the Gendarme of Europe. In 1849 he sent Russian troops to put down a rising against Austrian rule in Hungary.

◀ Nihilist prisoners leaving St Petersburg for Siberia,
November 1879

In the same year the police discovered that certain individuals in St Petersburg were meeting to discuss politics, an activity which the Tsar regarded as a criminal offence. It was hardly a revolutionary plot, but twenty-one of those involved received death sentences. On 22 December 1849, soldiers marched them into a public square in the capital to face a firing-squad. The executioners had actually levelled their muskets and were expecting the order to fire, when an official suddenly announced a change of sentence to imprisonment and exile. Nicholas himself had planned this cruel scene in order to teach potential Russian revolutionaries a lesson. The most celebrated victim of the ordeal was the novelist Fyodor Dostoyevsky, then a young radical, but later to become a pillar of extreme conservatism.

When Nicholas I died in 1855 there was a general feeling of relief. The passing of a harsh Emperor after thirty years of severe rule created the impression that better times might now begin, though Russia was facing defeat in the Crimean War against Great Britain, Turkey and France. The war had shown that Nicholas's rule was inefficient as well as cruel. His officials cared only for bribes, it seemed, and their failure to send adequate arms and supplies to the armies in the Crimea was a public scandal. Even some extreme conservatives now believed that the time had come for a change.

What most needed changing, as Nicholas I himself had known, was the position of the serfs. To keep about fifty million citizens in slavery in the mid-nineteenth century seemed a sign of backwardness as well as being outrageously inhumane. There was a feeling that Russia's primitive economic and social system, of which serfdom was the main feature, had caused her defeat in the Crimean War. Moreover, the serfs had taken to rioting on an increasing scale now that the stern Nicholas I was dead.

The new Tsar, Alexander II, accordingly announced that it was 'better to abolish serfdom from above than to wait for it to begin to abolish itself from below.' He meant that he himself must end serfdom, otherwise a full-scale peasant revolution might break out. Though he was a conservative in many ways, he persisted with his intention to liberate the peasants against strong opposition from many serfowners, and in 1861 he decreed the emancipation, or freedom, of all the serfs.

It has been said that the most dangerous time for a bad government is the moment when it starts to reform, and this seems to have been true in Russia. The emancipation of the serfs did not go far enough since it did not give the

Alexander II

peasants enough land and left many of them as poor as ever. But it was less among peasants than among intellectuals that the Russian revolutionary movement continued to find its main supporters. The revolutionaries of the 1860s and 1870s were often called Nihilists, a name given to them by the writer Turgenev in his novel *Fathers and Children*, since there was nothing (Latin *nihil*) which they would take on trust, and no authority to which they would submit.

Many Nihilists were or had been university students, and student demonstrations played a part in the unrest of the period. Nihilists also printed illegal proclamations demanding anything from a constitution to the shedding of rivers of blood and the murder of the Imperial Family. Many of

27

them thought that such violence would bring in an age of social justice, others advocated destruction for destruction's sake, while yet others were inspired by the spirit of adventure. One young Nihilist accosted the Tsar himself in the garden of his palace and handed him a Socialist pamphlet, and another charged down the Nevsky Prospekt in St Petersburg on a galloping horse, scattering illegal proclamations as he went.

Calls to violence were soon followed by violence itself. In 1866 a former student, who had been expelled from two universities, fired a revolver at the Tsar in the Summer Garden in St Petersburg. He missed—not many revolutionaries were good marksmen—and was tried and hanged. The incident discouraged Alexander II's reforming activities, but only after he had already modernised the law-courts and local government, besides abolishing the worst forms of flogging.

In the 1870s revolutionaries began to pay more attention to the peasants. Most of these were still poor and ill-treated, and it was believed that they would gladly rise against the Tsar's government and destroy it if only educated people would encourage them. Hundreds of young Nihilist men and women accordingly visited the villages. Some of them dressed up in smocks or sleeveless dresses called sarafans to make themselves look like the local inhabitants, as they tried to win the peasants for the revolutionary cause. But most of the peasants were devoted to the Tsar, much as they loathed his officials and their own landlords, and they viewed these middle-class agitators with the deepest suspicion.

These attempts to start a peasant revolution were a failure, and the police arrested many of the agitators, who were put on trial. At first the courts treated them leniently, but in 1878 a harsher phase began with the flogging of a revolutionary in gaol for refusing to remove his cap in the presence of an inspecting general. Soon afterwards a Nihilist girl decided to avenge this insult, and ambushed the general in his anteroom. When he appeared she took a revolver out of her muff and fired, but only wounded him.

This episode helped to spread the idea of political assassination among revolutionaries, their hope being that the murder of important members of the Tsar's administration would eventually cause the whole autocratic system to collapse. There was little prospect of success for this far-fetched plan, but terrorists killed several high officials by revolver and dagger, and then proceeded to attack the Tsar himself.

In 1879 members of a new terrorist group, People's Will, buried bombs

Police raid on a Nihilist printing press, St Petersburg, 1880

under railway lines over which Alexander's train was to travel on his way to St Petersburg from his residence in the Crimea. One bomb did not explode, however, and another struck the wrong train. In the following year the terrorists came nearer to success with a huge explosion beneath the dining-room of the Tsar's Winter Palace in St Petersburg. About fifty people died or were injured, mostly soldiers of the palace guard, but the Tsar himself escaped since he happened to be late for dinner on that evening.

Early in 1881 members of People's Will were plotting to kill the Tsar in the streets of his capital. They rented a cheese shop on the ground floor of a street along which Alexander's carriage regularly passed during visits to a cavalry parade-ground not far from his palace. From the basement they dug a tunnel under the road and planted high explosive.

On 1 March, the day chosen for the attempt, the Tsar happened to travel by another route, but on this occasion People's Will could fall back on a reserve plan, having stationed four young revolutionaries in the streets on the Tsar's route. Each of them carried a crudely constructed hand-grenade and they were under the tactical command of Sophia Perovsky, daughter

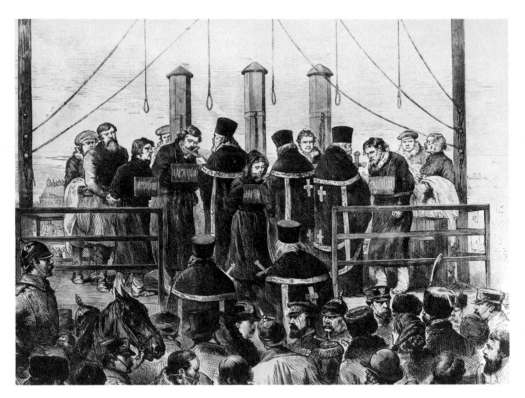

The execution of Alexander II's assassins

of a high official. As this illustrates, members of the middle and upper classes continued prominent in the revolutionary movement, and the women were often more active and ruthless than the young men.

Sophia used her troops effectively. Though the first grenade exploded under Alexander's carriage without hurting him, he made the mistake of climbing down and going back to investigate. Then a second assassin threw his bomb. It killed the Emperor and himself.

The assassination of Alexander II was a political failure since it only brought to the throne a more reactionary ruler in the dead Tsar's son, who now became Alexander III. He had five of his father's killers publicly hanged, and embarked on a programme of 'counter-reforms' designed to keep influence in the hands of the privileged classes. Amongst other things, he turned down a plan to give bodies partly and indirectly elected by the people the right to advise the Tsar. This would have been a very timid step towards representative government and a political constitution.

30

Revolutionary men of action could make little headway under Alexander III, and from 1881 onwards there was a lull in political terrorism which lasted for twenty years. The only important assassination plot of the period was a scheme to bomb the new Tsar on the anniversary of his father's death. As an added refinement the conspirators primed their grenades with strychnine pellets besides filling them with high explosive, but the police arrested them before they could go into action. One of those hanged for this offence was the elder brother of the great revolutionary Lenin. Lenin was seventeen years old at the time of his brother's execution, which he avenged over thirty years later—on Alexander's son Nicholas II, who came to the throne in 1894.

5

The Growth
of Revolutionary
Movements

Russian revolutionaries had continued to discuss their political theories in secret during the long lull in terrorist activity imposed under Alexander III, but when Nicholas II, a new and apparently a milder Tsar, succeeded to the throne, the time had come to think once again in terms of revolutionary action.

Most of the revolutionaries were Socialists, who believed that transport, land, factories and other means of production or sources of wealth should belong to the community as a whole—not to private individuals. As things developed, Russian Socialists were falling into two different camps, depending on what view they took of the peasants.

One trend of thought eventually led to the founding of the Socialist Revolutionary Party in 1902. Socialist Revolutionaries believed that the peasants held the key to the future. Peasants still formed about four-fifths of the population, and were still so poor and ill-treated that they must surely be ripe for rebellion. Moreover, Russian peasants had one custom which made them seem like Socialists of a kind already—many villagers managed their affairs and owned their land communally, not as individuals. It was argued that their village communes might offer Russia a short cut to Socialism not open to the more advanced countries of western Europe.

All this was so much dull theory. What most attracted attention to the

33

Socialist Revolutionaries was something more spectacular—their revival, on a far larger scale, of political terrorism as once practised by People's Will.

In 1901 the Minister of Education was shot, the first political murder of a reign in which assassination was soon to become commonplace. Shortly afterwards the Socialist Revolutionaries went on to murder two Ministers of the Interior within three years, which made them seem by far the most dangerous of the Russian revolutionary parties.

Meanwhile, however, a rival subversive party had also arisen, one which was to be far more successful in the long run than that of the Socialist Revolutionaries. It consisted of followers of Karl Marx, the celebrated German-Jewish political and economic thinker, who had died in 1883. Marx taught that there were two main classes in society. Firstly, there were the capitalists, or *bourgeois*, who owned the factories and other places of work. Secondly, there were the workers, or proletariat, hired by the capitalists to make money for them. Caring for nothing but profit, the capitalists were bound, in Marx's opinion, to exploit the workers with increasing ruthlessness as time went on, while they themselves became progressively richer. Eventually, the workers would carry through a violent revolution, seize all the means of production and set up a society in which there would be no classes and everyone would be content.

Marx was a materialist, believing the world to consist only of those things which people can touch and see—material objects such as houses, clothes, food, machines and tools, and he therefore rejected such intangible human motives as religious conviction or nationalism.

Marx advanced the theory of dialectical materialism, which explains all historical and other events as the outcome of a clash between conflicting forces. Thus feudalism had given way to capitalism, and capitalism in turn must eventually give way to a classless, proletarian society. Because of their belief that historical development is governed by such exact laws to which they alone hold the key, Marxists sometimes refer to themselves as 'scientific' Socialists.

In 1848 Marx explained some of his ideas in a short pamphlet, *The Communist Manifesto*, in which he wrote: 'Workers of the world unite, you have nothing to lose but your chains.' Later he also wrote a long book, *Capital*, a study of economics, but also the most celebrated revolutionary work ever written. It may seem surprising that the Russian censors of the 1870s allowed it to appear in Russia in Russian translation. However, Marx's few Russian followers seemed unimportant at this time, being

A workers' barracks at the end of the nineteenth century

apparently concerned only with obscure economic theories, and talking a mysterious jargon which others could not understand. Unlike Socialist Revolutionaries, Marxists did not practise political assassination, and therefore seemed less dangerous. But it was not because they were gentler than Socialist Revolutionaries that Marxists rejected terrorism. They did not object to shedding blood—but they happened to believe that isolated acts of terrorism would not be effective in bringing about revolution, besides which, in their view, revolution was inevitable in any case.

It was over the peasant question that Marxists most strongly disagreed with Socialist Revolutionaries. Marxists considered peasants to be political 'idiots', and pinned their hopes for revolution on the proletariat, the factory workers of the cities. Russian workers were not very numerous— there were only about three million of them at the beginning of the twentieth century, when peasants numbered about a hundred million.

However, Russian industry was now growing fast from tiny beginnings, and industrial workers were rapidly increasing in number.

The development of industry has brought ill-treatment to the workers in most countries, and Russian workers were no exception. They were forced to toil for long hours in dangerous and uncomfortable conditions. Their food was poor, their wages were low. Their housing often consisted of repulsive barracks provided by their employers, where many families huddled together in dirty, unhealthy dormitories. And though the government tried to improve labourers' conditions and limited hours of work by law, these regulations were often ignored—like many other Russian regulations. The workers took to striking for better conditions, and as Nicholas II's reign proceeded strikes became more common and more violent.

To put down strikes and workers' demonstrations the authorities used Cossacks, especially ferocious troops recruited in certain outlying areas of the Empire. They would charge rioting workers or students with whips and sabres, which was usually effective at the time, but did not make the government popular in the factories and universities.

The more the authorities ill-treated the workers, the more satisfied the Marxists were, because they felt that events were developing according to Marx's teaching, and that revolution was approaching. But they did not expect Russia to be the first country to have a workers' revolution, for Marx taught that such an outbreak must first occur in advanced industrial countries such as Britain and Germany. Only after that could it spread to a comparatively backward country like Russia.

In addition many Russian Marxists insisted that the workers' revolution must be preceded in their country by a *bourgeois* revolution—one in which the middle class would seize power from the autocracy. Then there would be a second, proletarian, revolution in which the workers would overthrow the *bourgeoisie*. These processes might take many years, and most Marxists therefore thought of revolution as a distant prospect.

In 1898, Russian Marxists set up their own secret political party—the Russian Social Democrat Labour Party, forerunner of the Communist Party of the Soviet Union. By this time Marx's ideas had attracted one young Russian who was soon to become the most famous revolutionary in history—Vladimir Ilyich Ulyanov. Like many revolutionaries, he took to using pseudonyms for his political work in order to confuse the police, and one of these, Lenin, is the name under which he became well known.

Lenin was born in 1870 in Simbirsk, a provincial town on the Volga. He was not himself a proletarian since his father belonged to the class of gentry, having risen from humble beginnings to become a high official in the education department of his province. A photograph of the Ulyanovs

The Ulyanov family, Vladimir, who later took the pseudonym Lenin, is seated at the bottom right

37

in the 1880s shows a conventional Russian middle-class family. But the impression is misleading, as is shown by the execution of Lenin's elder brother Alexander for political terrorism.

Lenin was soon deep in revolutionary activity on his own account. The authorities expelled him from Kazan University, where he was studying law. He took his degree, however, and in 1893 he moved to St Petersburg, where he was active in secret Marxist discussion circles. In 1895 he was arrested, and spent the next five years in prison and in exile in southern Siberia, where he married a girl, Nadezhda Krupsky, who shared his own views, and who was to help him with his work. He also wrote a book on the development of capitalism in Russia and went duck shooting in the marshes. Soon after his release he left Russia to work for a Russian revolution abroad.

Lenin is one of the most remarkable figures in history. He was a frugal man of simple habits—a typical Russian intellectual, it has been said—and seemed to lack all personal ambition. But he was utterly single-minded in pursuing the cause of revolution. Where revolution was concerned he was always sure that he knew best, and he was also firmly convinced that anyone who disagreed with him should not be allowed to express himself at all if there was any way to silence him. He was modest and retiring in his personal life, but completely ruthless where politics were concerned.

Few *émigré* Russian revolutionaries much resembled the future rulers of a great nation. They seemed more like over-excitable eccentrics. Lenin dominated some of them, and he tried to put those he could not dominate at a disadvantage by ingenious tactics. In 1903 he helped to cause a split in the Social Democrat Party at a congress held in London. There was a disagreement about what sort of individuals should be allowed to become Party members. Lenin conceived the Party as a small band of professional revolutionaries utterly dedicated to revolution—by which he privately meant to himself personally. Others preferred a larger and looser organisation. The Social Democrats who agreed with Lenin took the name of Bolsheviks—those of the majority. Their opponents who favoured a larger organisation were called Mensheviks—those of the minority. There was a bitter feud between the two camps. But not all was harmony within them either, and Lenin was continually quarrelling with his own supporters, while all the time trying to weld a compact group loyal to himself. He preferred to be surrounded by a few men who would carry out his orders rather than by large numbers of vague supporters who were liable to argue and disagree.

Since the words revolutionary, Marxist, Socialist, Social Democrat, Bolshevik and Communist can be confusing, it may be helpful to state that Lenin considered himself all these things. However, he was above all a practical planner of revolution rather than a theorist, and he was ready to adopt any label and any tactics likely to gain him power. He was well content for his followers to increase Party funds by criminal means or sharp practice. Some, for instance, carried out bank robberies in Russia. Others married rich heiresses so that they could obtain possession of their money and use it for the revolutionary cause. But Lenin did not take part in such operations himself, and it would never have occurred to him to keep any of the proceeds for his private use. All was for the revolution.

6

Nicholas II

In May 1896, during the celebrations of Nicholas II's coronation in Moscow, a large crowd gathered in the Khodynka Field near the city to receive from the Tsar certain customary gifts, including mugs carrying the Imperial crest. Somehow the people began jostling, and panic broke out. They were so tightly packed together that they trampled on each other, and over twelve hundred men, women and children died in the stampede. Nicholas was not there himself, and the police were more to blame than the Emperor for the disaster. But on the same evening Emperor and Empress unwisely attended a ball given by the French ambassador, which made them seem more callous than they really were.

The catastrophe of Khodynka helped to discredit Nicholas with his subjects, including many who were by no means revolutionaries. By the beginning of the twentieth century most educated Russians had come to regard the Tsar and the complicated ritual of his court as hopelessly out of date. Nicholas's father had at least been a big burly man who looked like an Emperor, but even that could not be said of the new Tsar. He was charming, polite and of pleasant appearance, but small and unimposing. He seemed more like a country squire than an autocrat, and apparently preferred playing with his dogs and children to governing his Empire. However, he had a strong sense of duty, and was determined to do God's

◄ Nicholas II and his wife, the Empress Alexandra, shortly after their marriage in 1894 will by reigning as a true autocrat. He made this clear early in his reign when it was proposed that more people ought to have some say in government. Nicholas firmly turned down such suggestions, and called them 'mad dreams'.

Ten years after Nicholas II's accession the need for a reform of the autocratic system was further emphasised by the war which broke out between Russia and Japan in 1904 as a result of rivalry between the two countries for control over Korea. Supporters of the Russian autocracy at first welcomed the war. They believed that the Russian Empire would easily defeat a small Asian people such as the Japanese, and that the war would turn Russians' attention away from their grievances at home, uniting them behind the Tsar as good patriots. However, Japan surprised the world by defeating Russia decisively on land and sea. This seemed to prove the inefficiency of the Imperial political system more convincingly than ever. The war against Japan weakened the Tsar, and thus helped to cause the first large-scale revolution in Russian history—that of 1905, in which year Russia signed peace with Japan.

Father Gapon, an Orthodox priest who was the leader of a trade union operating under police protection, started the 1905 revolution unintentionally. He organised a mass demonstration in St Petersburg on 9 January—his plan being to march workers from all over the capital to the square in front of the Winter Palace, where they would kneel while Gapon himself solemnly handed to the Tsar a petition on their behalf. This petition included a demand for a constitution, but its style was humble, and the general mood of the marchers was more suitable for a picnic than for a revolution. They had their wives and children with them, and carried portraits of the Tsar and icons as a sign that they were still loyal to Nicholas and to the Church. As they marched along singing hymns, they could not foresee that the outing would end as 'Bloody Sunday'.

The authorities were warned of the demonstration in advance by Gapon himself, and set up on the approaches to the Palace Square barriers manned by Cossacks and other troops. But the people still pressed on when ordered to turn back. Troops opened fire with rifles, and Cossacks charged, swinging their whips. Some demonstrators forced a way through to the Palace Square, only to be shot down there. The troops killed over a hundred people, while Gapon himself slipped away without being able to present his petition to the Tsar, who was in any case not in residence at the time. The Minister of the Interior and the police had failed to control the crowds

Bloody Sunday: a peaceful procession

properly, but it was the mild and well-meaning Nicholas himself who received most of the blame and even the nickname Nicholas the Bloody.

Bloody Sunday provoked strikes in factories in many parts of the country, while villagers in widespread areas took up their old tradition of rioting, looting and burning. In June, revolutionary sailors of the Black Sea Fleet seized a battleship, the *Potemkin*, from their officers. By October all the railwaymen of the Empire were out on strike, and soon the strike became general throughout the country. It paralysed the whole Empire, closed the banks, and stopped the newspapers and mail. Teachers and other professional people, even some ballet dancers, came out in sympathy with the workers, and liberals made common cause with revolutionaries—as did several army and navy units in addition to the *Potemkin*'s crew. So did many of the non-Russian peoples living on the frontiers of the Empire, including Poles, Finns, Jews, Caucasians and Balts.

It was not an organised revolution, and had taken the main revolutionary leaders by surprise at a time when many of them were abroad. In October

43

Bloody Sunday: an artist's impression of the
scene before the Winter Palace

some of them tried to control the chaotic upheaval by helping to set up in
the capital an assembly of workers' representatives—the St Petersburg
Soviet. But 'soviet' is only the ordinary Russian word for a council and in
1905 few could guess that it would ever give a name to a new system of
government and to the country as a whole. In the St Petersburg Soviet of
1905 the Mensheviks were the most influential group, but Leo Trotsky was
the dominant figure. A brilliant young revolutionary of Jewish origin who
had escaped from exile in Siberia, he was neither a Menshevik nor a Bolshevik, and was opposed during his early political career to Lenin's dictatorial
tendencies. He overshadowed Lenin at this time, though Lenin did return
to Russia briefly in November.

The St Petersburg Soviet achieved little, and its importance was mainly
as a symbol of workers' power. But by now the workers themselves were
fast losing enthusiasm. A general reaction against violence had set in, and
on 3 December the government felt strong enough to move against the
St Petersburg Soviet, and arrest its members after it had provided a kind

44

of rival administration for fifty days. However, Moscow too had a Soviet, one in which the Bolsheviks were stronger, and on 10 December it launched an armed uprising. Troops put down this suicidal last stand in a week, using artillery to win unequal street battles in which they massacred poorly armed workers and their sympathisers.

Though the revolution of 1905 failed, the revolutionaries had tasted blood, and had even had a foretaste of political power. Moreover, Nicholas did now grant some political concessions, allowing the election of a State Duma. This body in some ways resembled a parliament, but one with very limited powers. Citizens did not receive equal votes in elections to the Duma, for groups thought to be friendly to the Tsar, such as property-owners, were given more representation than others. The Duma might propose measures, but it could not always carry them through since there was an upper house which could veto its decisions. So could the Tsar him-

Members of the St Petersburg Soviet arrested in
December 1905. Trotsky is second from left

45

self. Moreover, he insisted on keeping the official name of Autocrat, which had been part of the Tsars' formal title for hundreds of years. Technically, however, he was a full autocrat no longer, for the new laws did at last give Russia the elements of a constitution.

The defeat of the 1905 revolution failed to halt the campaign of assassination pursued by the Socialist Revolutionaries. In the two years 1906–7 terrorists murdered over four thousand people—state officials

Peter Stolypin

46

from generals to village policemen. The assassins did not go unpunished, however. Nicholas now had in Peter Stolypin a President of the Council of Ministers—Prime Minister, in effect—who was determined to restore order. The authorities imposed martial law in many areas, and set up courts martial. By executing several hundred persons and sending punitive expeditions to the worst trouble spots, they re-established peace and quiet by the end of 1907. In any case people were now weary of violent excesses, and revolutionary activity went into a decline while Stolypin tried to strengthen the Imperial government in various ways. Believing that Russia needed energetic, independent farmers in place of her traditional down-trodden peasants, he made it possible for villagers to leave their communes and own their farms individually. But after a few years Stolypin himself was assassinated—in 1911 at a gala performance in the opera house at Kiev in southern Russia, and in the presence of the Tsar. He was shot by a revolutionary who was an agent of the police.

By now a complicated situation had developed in the revolutionary and counter-revolutionary worlds. In order to spy out plans against them, revolutionaries would enlist in the police, while plain-clothes police agents

The Duma in session

47

were in turn enrolling as revolutionaries. Both kinds of infiltrator had to lead a double life, but that was only the beginning. For instance, a police agent pretending to be a revolutionary might play his part so well that he became a genuine believer in Socialism, perhaps without noticing it, while still reporting to the police as a police agent. Then he might change his mind again so that he had become first an agent, then a double agent, then a triple and quadruple agent, and so on. Some of these individuals were unbalanced in the first place, and in course of time they grew so confused that it is not always possible for historians to be sure which side they really supported. In some cases they may even not have been clear about this themselves, and Stolypin's assassin, Bogrov, was probably such a man.

This sort of confusion helped to undermine authority and to create a situation in which the violent overthrow of the state became a more likely prospect.

7

World War I

In the summer of 1914 the First World War broke out between Russia (whose allies included Great Britain and France) and the Central Powers —Germany, Austria, Turkey and Bulgaria. The general causes of the war lay in competing national ambitions, and the immediate cause of Russia's involvement was the support which she gave to her fellow-Slavs, the Serbians, when they were threatened by Austria with Germany's encouragement.

By this time the prospects for a Russian revolution seemed remote, partly because the country had made great economic advances during Nicholas's reign, and the standard of living had risen. Though the Duma possessed little power and was never a real parliament, many people had the impression that gradual reform might continue and might suit the country better than a sudden, violent upheaval such as that of 1905.

By contrast with the Russo-Japanese War, which had never been popular, war with Germany united the nation behind the Tsar in a wave of patriotic enthusiasm. The Duma itself, though often critical of the government, staged a loyal demonstration when it met just after the outbreak of hostilities. In this mood of nationalism the name of the capital city was changed to Petrograd to give it a more Russian sound, and even Russian revolutionary leaders hoped for a Russian victory—though the Bolsheviks,

49

Russian prisoners of war in Austria after the Battle of Tannenberg, August 1914

not yet a large or important group, were among the exceptions. They
expected that a Russian defeat would bring the revolution nearer.

Harmonious relations between Tsar and people did not long outlast the
autumn of 1914, one reason being military defeat in the west. Russian
soldiers were brave, but even the best troops cannot fight well if they have
no boots or rifles, as was sometimes the case. Mistakes in generalship, and
defects in training and preparation, also help to explain why the Russians
sustained crushing defeats by the well-prepared German armies on the
Russian western front in 1914–15. These included the Battle of Tannenberg
in late August 1914, when General von Hindenburg routed the Russian
General Samsonov, destroying the whole Russian Second Army. German
troops advanced into Poland and occupied other large areas in the west of
the Russian Empire, while Russia sustained enormous losses on the fronts.
The war also brought a sharp rise in prices inside the country together with
a shortage of food caused partly by the fact that so many peasants had been
called up into the army.

It might have been easier to bear these hardships if they had not appeared to be the fault of the autocratic system. Members of the Duma and of other public bodies were eager to play their part in winning the war, but the Tsar and his Ministers would not allow them to contribute as much as they wished. Nevertheless, various organisations outside the government—including a Duma committee, trade unions, local government councils and businessmen—did co-operate with each other to improve such things as arms production and supply, to the point where a kind of shadow administration was growing up alongside government by the Tsar and his Ministers. Between these organisations and the government there was constant friction and ill will.

In August 1915 the Tsar took a decision which aroused further criticism by assuming supreme command of the Russian armed forces. He had not been neglecting military affairs, for as a monarch with a strong sense of duty he had frequently visited his fighting troops and conferred with his generals. And though he now felt that he must have an official position as the overall commander, he intended only to be a figurehead—having no experience of commanding army formations in battle; he left that to his Chief of Staff. But many of his closest supporters considered his assumption of supreme command inadvisable, since the blame for any new Russian defeats in the west would fall on the Tsar personally and thus further discredit the autocratic system.

8

The Imperial Family
and Rasputin

As it happened, Russia made better progress in the war under her new Commander-in-Chief, and the year 1916 saw some Russian military successes in the west. However, the decline in the Tsar's popularity continued, for reasons connected with his family life. His wife, the Empress Alexandra, had been a German princess. She was beautiful, pious and strong-willed, but unfortunately had little judgement. She surrounded herself with various eccentric protégés who discussed religion with her, and being somewhat reserved by nature she did not greatly enjoy company apart from these few people and members of her own family. This earned her the dislike of court circles, and eventually her unpopularity spread far beyond them. But Nicholas adored his wife in spite of her faults.

There was a desperate need for a male heir to inherit a throne from which females had been legally barred for over a century, but unluckily Alexandra seemed able to give birth only to girls. At last, in 1904, a boy was born— Tsarevich (son of a Tsar) Alexis. Soon, however, the parents began to wonder whether their son would ever live to be Tsar, for it was discovered that he suffered from the hereditary disease of haemophilia, transmitted by his mother. This meant that if he cut or bruised himself and began to bleed, the flow of blood would not stop. There was no cure for the disease, though hypnosis could sometimes stop the attacks.

◄ The Imperial Family shortly after the
birth of the Tsarevich Alexis

By another stroke of ill luck for the Russian royal line, the only person who could relieve the Tsarevich's attacks, presumably by hypnosis, was Gregory Rasputin—a disreputable and repulsive Siberian peasant with staring eyes and a mysterious ability to dominate others. He was not a

Gregory Rasputin

monk, as was sometimes believed, but was fond of making solemn pronouncements of a religious nature. The Empress Alexandra liked to associate with such people in any case, and she fell even more deeply under Rasputin's influence when she discovered that he could apparently save the life of her son.

Rasputin was boastful and dirty. He sometimes removed his clothes in public, and was often drunk. But in spite of his many bad habits and unpleasant appearance it was even whispered that the Empress was infatuated with him, and though this was untrue, there are some situations in which false rumours can have much the same effect as if they were based on fact. People also believed, and with more reason, that Rasputin influenced the appointment of ministers, a matter in which Alexandra began to have more say after her husband had made himself Commander-in-Chief and was often absent at the front. Ministers were still being appointed and dismissed at the whim of the Tsar. If, as was commonly thought, Nicholas had increasingly made this power over to Alexandra, and she in turn to the eccentric Rasputin, that might explain why the Imperial choice often fell on such unsuitable ministers. It might also explain why individual ministers were appointed and dismissed so rapidly that the phrase 'ministerial leap-frog' was coined. Once again, rumour exaggerated all these matters, and Rasputin certainly had less influence on policy than was commonly believed. He was not the centre of a conspiratorial 'black bloc' of traitorous 'dark forces', as was supposed, although he looked sinister enough for such a part. Still less was he an agent of the German enemy helping to send Russia to her doom through an Empress who had been born a German, it was now remembered, and might be plotting to betray Russia to the German Kaiser. Unfortunately this slander was widely believed, and the slogan 'Down with the German woman' began to be repeated.

Revolutionaries did not greatly object to Rasputin, who was useful to them because he brought discredit on the Tsar. It was among conservatives, patriots and supporters of the war effort that much of the indignation arose, since they felt that the scandal was undermining the autocracy, and after various attempts to remove Rasputin by gentler means had failed, three highly-placed personages decided to kill him. They were Prince Felix Yusupov, the Grand Duke Dmitry (a nephew of the Tsar) and Purishkevich, (a right-wing deputy of the Duma). These assassins had to feed Rasputin quantities of poisoned cakes and wine, shoot him with a revolver and then drown him before he finally died.

Others besides Rasputin and revolutionaries were also engaged in throwing discredit, directly or indirectly, on the Tsar during the war. On 1 November 1916 the liberal leader Paul Milyukov made a famous speech in which he practically accused the Empress of being a German agent. Thousands of copies of the speech were passed around, and helped to condemn Nicholas and Alexandra in the eyes of the public on the eve of the revolutionary year 1917.

9

The February Revolution

Two Russian revolutions took place in 1917—the first in February and the second in October. According to the dates used in western Europe, these events occurred in March and November respectively since the calendar used in Russia at this time lagged thirteen days behind that of Europe in general. For instance, 8 March 1917 in London and Paris was 23 February in Petrograd. It was on this date that the February Revolution began.

By early 1917 most Russians, whether soldiers or civilians, were utterly weary of war, and they had learnt to blame the Tsar for every disaster. Few observers, however, expected a revolution to break out at this particular time, and members of the revolutionary parties were taken as much by surprise as anyone else. Many revolutionary leaders were still abroad—for instance, Lenin was in Zürich and Trotsky was in the Bronx, in New York City. Others, including Stalin, were in exile in Siberia.

These leaders took no part in planning the details of the February Revolution, for it was not a planned *coup*—simply a collapse of authority. Even after it had started, the leading revolutionaries were unable to steer it effectively since the pace of events was too swift. This was a nine-day wonder—literally so since it began on 23 February, with strikes and riots on the streets of Petrograd, and ended on 3 March, the day on which it became clear that no Tsar was ever likely to rule Russia again.

Since the Tsar himself was absent from Petrograd at the time, the Revolution resembled a play with a few main parts acted by understudies, but consisting mainly of crowd scenes. Petrograd was the stage, and almost the only one. With a few minor exceptions the rest of the country remained quiet, and many inhabitants of the provinces did not even realise that a revolution was taking place until news of it reached them by telegram.

This historic upheaval began on 23 February with rioting in the queues at bakers' shops in Petrograd, where there was some local shortage of bread, but no threat of famine. On the same day nearly a hundred thousand workers happened to be on strike or locked out by their employers. Many of them surged into the streets and added to the uproar caused by the bread rioters—and also by the celebration of International Women's Day. Some demonstrators bore red flags or banners carrying the slogans 'We want bread!' 'Down with the war!' and 'Down with the autocracy!' They shouted these and other catch-words, sang revolutionary songs and listened to the hoarse bellowing of street-corner orators. Some clashes occurred between rioters and police, but there was nothing unusual in that—Petrograd had known such scenes before.

Similar incidents occurred on the following day, but on a larger scale. Twice as many workers were out on strike, and the rioters decided to push through to the centre of the city from the working-class districts north of the River Neva. Though the police blocked the bridges, nothing effective was done to stop the crowds when they began to make their way over the ice of the frozen river. In the city centre rioting workers joined forces with members of the middle class, including civil servants, teachers and students such as were often prominent in Russian political disturbances. Fighting broke out between crowds and police in which rioters used any weapon that came to hand—sticks, cobble-stones, lumps of ice and bottles. At this stage, however, police and riot troops were probably under orders not to fire except in self-defence, and the general mood of both sides remained good-humoured.

The third day, 25 February, saw more incidents of the same kind, but pitched at a higher level of excitement. The strike had now become general, and policemen were afraid to appear on the streets in some parts of the city. Most significant of all, there were signs that the troops might be siding with the crowds. Not that there was any battle line between the two, for no serious attempts were made to barricade the city streets, as commonly happens in revolutions. On the contrary, enemies and defenders of the

A food queue in Petrograd, 1917

existing order rubbed shoulders with each other, and with the thronging sight-seers who were not committed to either side but found the situation exhilarating even if they could not understand it.

One of the most important incidents of 25 February occurred at the eastern end of the Nevsky Prospekt, in Znamensky Square. This had become a favourite site for demonstrations, and the usual large crowd had gathered there to listen to revolutionary speeches delivered from the base of the equestrian statue of Alexander III. Members of a Cossack unit stood by watching, but did nothing to interfere. Then a police lieutenant suddenly rode up at the head of a detachment of men and pushed his way through the crowd to seize the red flag near the speaker—the usual first move in breaking up a demonstration. What happened next is not entirely clear, but according to one version a Cossack trooper turned on the police

Street scene, Petrograd, 1917

officer and cut him down with his sabre. In any case the officer was murdered—and, it was believed, by Cossacks who seemed ready to join the rioters. For years the government had relied on these hardened riot squadrons to control unruly mobs with their whips and sabres. The situation must indeed be growing desperate if even the Cossacks' loyalty could no longer be assumed.

This was the impression which the Emperor Nicholas was now forming at his Army General Headquarters in Mogilyov about four hundred miles south of Petrograd. For reports about his capital he relied on telegrams from his officials. They tried to play down the importance of what was happening, as also did the Empress Alexandra, who was not far from Petrograd in the Imperial palace of Tsarskoye Selo. She wrote to Nicholas on 25 February that this was only a movement of hooligans who would 'all stay at home if the weather was very cold'—which, as it happened, it actually was. The British Ambassador to Petrograd had telegraphed to his government that there were 'some disorders, but nothing serious'.

Nicholas, however, sensed that the disorders might be more dangerous than his advisers suggested. He telegraphed on 25 February to General Khabalov, Commander of the Petrograd Military District, ordering him to suppress all disturbances on the following day. Khabalov accordingly instructed his troops to fire on the crowds if they would not break up after due warning—an order which did more than anything else to turn riots into revolution. The Petrograd garrison, consisting of about 160,000 troops, should have been able to put down the disturbances easily. But though some units had been specially organised to deal with an emergency such as had developed, they were of generally poor quality and their morale was low. And what if the troops themselves should rebel? For that possibility the authorities had made no preparations.

On Sunday 26 February, however, the new tactics apparently proved their worth. Soldiers fired their rifles at the crowds in several parts of Petrograd. On Znamensky Square, that favourite trouble spot, men of the Volhynian Regiment opened up with machine-guns and killed forty people. But though order had apparently been restored, the instruction to shoot at unarmed crowds soon recoiled on the authorities' own heads. Discussing the massacre in their barracks that night, the Volhynians were disgusted at what they had been ordered to do, and these very soldiers were among the first to mutiny on the following day, 27 February.

The military revolt quickly spread through unit after unit of the Petrograd garrison as soldiers tumbled out of their barracks in an unruly mob, throwing away their rifles, firing them off at random, or selling them to civilian rioters. Pinning scraps of red ribbon on their grey military greatcoats to show that they had joined the revolution, some of them went from barracks to barracks calling on other regiments to mutiny as well. By no means all units obeyed the call, but those which remained loyal were badly led and undecided, and though some officers succeeded in rallying their men, others were shot by their own troops or went into hiding.

Armed civilians in peaked caps, cloth caps or bowler hats mingled with soldiers in their grey greatcoats to swell the revolutionary mobs. All were in holiday mood as they broke up police stations, burnt law-courts, burst into the gaols to free common criminals along with political prisoners, rode around the city in trucks with rifles levelled hoping to find enemies of the revolution, fired off salvoes at random, overturned trams, and raided the arsenals for weapons, while shouting revolutionary songs and generally expressing their high spirits. Placards, slogans, red ribbons, red flags and

61

red banners were to be seen on all sides, and the mob ransacked cellars and attics for policemen, who were especially detested because of a rumour that they had been sniping at the crowds from roof-tops. Some of the police would have been glad to surrender to a proper revolutionary authority, but where was such an authority to be found?

Meanwhile certain last-minute attempts were being made to assert the Tsar's shaken authority. Prince Golitsyn, the Chairman of the Council of Ministers, released an order—signed by Nicholas and held in reserve until this time—proroguing the Duma. But this ban did not prevent Duma members from continuing to meet, technically as private individuals, in another part of the building which was their headquarters—the Tauris Palace, once built by Catherine the Great for her favourite, Prince Potemkin. Then General Khabalov made a last desperate bid to quell the revolution by issuing a declaration of martial law. It turned out, however, that no glue was available to stick up his proclamations, and he had them scattered about the streets—where they were blown around in the wind and trampled underfoot in the dirty snow.

The Council of Ministers—that is to say, the Tsar's government—met on the night of 27 February in the Maryinsky Palace, and dispersed when the electric light failed. The ministers did not formally give up office, but they were never to meet again. On the same night the crowds looted the Maryinsky Palace, and soon afterwards most of the ministers were in hiding or under arrest. By midnight on 27–8 February all organised resistance by the Tsar's government had collapsed in Petrograd. It did not follow, however, that organised revolutionary leadership had taken its place.

In the small hours of 28 February the Tsar left Mogilyov by train for his palace at Tsarskoye Selo, about fifteen miles from the capital city where, had he but known it, he was no longer master. He wished to be near Petrograd, and also to join his wife and family at the palace—he was worried because his children were suffering from measles. But the Imperial trains made slow progress in the chaotic conditions of the railway line. The Emperor was still about a hundred miles south of Petrograd twenty-four hours after leaving Mogilyov, when he learnt that the track ahead of him was in revolutionary hands. He decided to turn back and make for Pskov, about a hundred and fifty miles south-west of the capital. There he should at least be safe from revolutionaries since it was at Pskov that his army had its northern headquarters.

On reaching Pskov late on the evening of 1 March, Nicholas discovered

◄ A demonstration before the Winter Palace, February 1917

that others besides revolutionary workers, soldiers and students wished to see his government overthrown. Even his generals now politely told him, or informed him by telegram, that drastic change was necessary. The Emperor first agreed to grant the Duma the power to form a government, which would have left him on the throne as a constitutional monarch. Further pressure persuaded him to abdicate in favour of his son, the Tsarevich Alexis, for whom the Grand Duke Michael, the boy's uncle and Nicholas's brother, was to act as regent. However, Nicholas's final decision, taken after he had talked to his doctor, was that he would not burden his invalid son with the cares of empire. In the Imperial train on a siding in Pskov station on the evening of 2 March the Tsar eventually signed a deed of abdication, assigning the throne directly to the Grand Duke Michael.

By this time, however, revolutionary excitement and hatred of the autocracy had reached such a pitch in the capital that the Grand Duke was persuaded to refuse so dangerous a crown. This decision, taken on 3 March 1917 in the Grand Duke's apartment in Petrograd, marked the end of a monarchy which traced its origin back over a thousand years into the mists of early Russian history. Its last representative, the ex-Tsar now called Nicholas Romanov, was held under arrest in his palace at Tsarskoye Selo with his family for several months, after which they were taken to Siberia.

10

The Provisional Government and the Soviet

Who was to rule Russia now that rule by Tsars had ended? The old system had collapsed so suddenly that it was necessary to make new arrangements with great speed, and some members of the Duma reacted to the crisis by choosing a cabinet of ministers from among their own leading members, chiefly liberals. The Prime Minister was Prince George Lvov, and one important figure was Paul Milyukov, leader of the main liberal party, who now became Foreign Minister.

The new government formally assumed office on 3 March, but it had no proper title to rule, for though the Grand Duke Michael had solemnly invested it with 'full powers' in his abdication manifesto, he had no legal right to bestow such powers. The Grand Duke's manifesto also described the new government as provisional, and stated that it should hold office only until the election of a Constituent Assembly—that is, of an entirely new body charged with drawing up a constitution and working out a permanent form of government. As for the Duma itself, that now ceased to have any effective existence.

Lacking full authority from the beginning, the Provisional Government even had to share the Tauris Palace, where it held its meetings, with a kind of rival administration—one which constantly interfered with government while itself refusing to govern. This was the Petrograd Soviet of Workers'

and Soldiers' Deputies, set up on a rough and ready basis in memory of the 1905 Revolution by Duma leaders belonging to the revolutionary parties and other politicians of the left. Mensheviks and Socialist Revolutionaries dominated its proceedings. The Bolsheviks were present in the Soviet too, but could not yet expect to play an important role since they were still a very small party. Soviets with roughly similar composition were also set up in Moscow and elsewhere throughout the country.

The Petrograd Soviet and the Provisional Government were on bad terms, for this was a partnership between natural enemies at best, and at worst a bitter feud. Though the Soviet had agreed to the establishment of the Provisional Government in the first place, it had done so grudgingly. Members of the Soviet had not themselves been ready to serve as ministers with one important exception in the new Minister of Justice—Alexander Kerensky, a revolutionary and the leader of the Labourists, a small left-wing party in the Duma. One reason why other members of the Soviet did not wish to accept office was the Marxist theory that a proletarian, or lower-class, revolution was impossible until a *bourgeois*, or middle-class, revolution had taken place first. They thought, in other words, that they must endure a period of rule by the liberal and middle-class politicians of the Provisional Government until a second, proletarian, revolution should sweep people such as themselves to power as representatives of the soldiers, workers and peasants.

Meanwhile the Soviet intended to supervise the activities of the Provisional Government and ensure that it did not betray the achievements of the revolution. This meant that the Provisional Government was never fully in power, especially since large sections of the population looked to the Soviet as the real authority. By its very nature the Soviet was difficult to work with, consisting as it did of nearly three thousand members elected on a haphazard basis by factories and military units. Delegates were liable to be recalled and replaced by others at short notice, and in any case initiative did not lie with the large, unwieldy Soviet as a whole, but with its Executive Committee—later expanded to include representatives of the provincial Soviets.

In these early days of revolution the corridors of the Tauris Palace rang by day and by night with the boots of enthusiastic soldiers and workers who had no real business there, but wanted to feel that they were part of history, even if Russia still had no proper government, but two half-governments of which neither possessed proper legal authority.

67

To maintain order, all governments depend on their police, and in the last resort on their soldiers. But shortly after the February Revolution the unpopular police force of Tsarist times had disappeared from the scene. Nor could the Provisional Government depend on the armed forces, for it was to the Soviet that the troops sent delegates, and it was to the Soviet that they looked for a lead rather than to their own officers or to the Government.

The Soviet encouraged this tendency with a proclamation, Order Number One, issued on 1 March. It provided for the establishment of committees of soldiers and sailors to control arms and equipment, preventing them from being issued to officers. Other provisions were more trivial. Troops need no longer salute off duty, or stand to attention when addressing their officers. The officers were not to receive such titles as 'your honour' any more, or to call their men 'thou' as if they were children or servants. Various later decrees changed or expanded Order Number One, and their general effect was to loosen military discipline already badly shaken by the February Revolution. There was also great danger in one particular arrangement supported by the Soviet—a guarantee to the troops of the Petrograd garrison that they would not be sent to the front. The result was that members of this huge force, many of whom had helped to make the February Revolution, were likely to spend much of their time at disorderly political meetings and thus increase the atmosphere of chaos in the capital.

Meanwhile Russia was still involved in a major war, which the Provisional Government had undertaken to win, against Germany, Austria and their allies. Though the collapse of Russian military discipline had infected the front-line troops, the German and Austrian generals did not press this advantage, seeming content to mark time. Meanwhile Russian soldiers at the front showed more interest in political agitation than in manning their trenches and weapons. Morale collapsed as they fell under the spell of revolutionary orators and fraternised with the enemy. Some lynched their officers, and they deserted in ever-increasing numbers. The sailors were even more unruly. During the February Revolution, when most of the country outside Petrograd remained calm, revolutionary sailors at the near-by naval base of Kronstadt had killed an admiral and forty officers. For these reasons it seemed that the armed forces might well turn against the Provisional Government in any crisis.

There were also problems for the Provisional Government in the country-side. Most Russian soldiers were peasants in uniform, and the chaos of the age was infecting the soldiers' village homes. The traditional lootings, burnings and lynchings flared up violently, besides which peasants now

Soldiers in the trenches on the Russian western front

felt free to take possession of the large privately owned estates and share out the land among themselves. Hearing of this, peasant soldiers at the front became all the more eager to desert and hurry home to seize land while there was still some available. It had been widely agreed for some time that the peasants needed more land, and the Provisional Government had set up a commission to study the problem. But at this point people wanted action, not more talk.

A feature of all these trends was a general move to the political left—that is to the further abandoning of all traditional restraints and also to the confiscation of industrial plant, landed property and capital from private individuals. So strong was this leftwards movement that crowds sometimes howled down spokesmen of the Bolsheviks because even they occasionally urged caution and seemed too tame for the inflamed revolutionary mobs.

With authority of every kind discredited or overthrown, February to October 1917 was the period of greatest freedom in Russia's history, but it was also a period of growing chaos which seemed to bode ill for the future.

11
Lenin's Return

In this bewildering situation there seemed to be no leader with clear-cut
policies—until, on 3 April, Lenin arrived by train from abroad at the
Finland Station in Petrograd. He had come to bring about a second
Russian revolution which should sweep himself and his party to power.

At the beginning of the World War in 1914 Lenin had been living on
Austro-Hungarian territory. The Austrian authorities arrested him as a
Russian spy, but then released him and permitted him to go to neutral
Switzerland. He did not allow the war to hamper his political activity—
indeed, opposition to the war now became a main item in his programme.
In peace time other European Socialists had also opposed war, but when
hostilities broke out many of them were infected by the patriotic enthusiasm of their own countries. To Lenin, however, this remained an imperialist
war between rival groups of capitalists. In his opinion there was little to
choose between the two sides, but he believed that the defeat of Imperial
Russia would suit his purposes better than the defeat of any other warring
power. He was prepared to work for the downfall of his own country,
believing as he did that world war offered an excellent opportunity to
bring about world revolution. He also believed that he could turn the struggle between nations into a mighty class struggle, with working people in all
countries banding together to fight against their capitalist rulers.

About the immediate future, however, Lenin was less hopeful. As late as 22 January 1917 he had made a speech to a Socialist youth meeting in Zürich, saying: 'We of the older generation may not live to see the decisive battles of the coming revolution.' When these words were spoken, Russia was still ruled by an Emperor who, within ten months, was destined to become the prisoner of Lenin—the first head of a Soviet Government. Nothing, however, could have seemed less likely in early 1917—if not to Lenin himself, then to the citizens of Zürich, where this little man with his unusual political views was living quietly with his wife in the house of a shoemaker. He did not look like the successor to a dynasty of autocrats. But even less did he resemble a typical *émigré* Russian revolutionary politician, being modest, hard-working and disciplined, with none of the eccentric personal habits which the prim Swiss had learnt to associate with Russian political exiles.

When news of the February Revolution reached Zürich, Lenin longed to return to Russia at once. But how could he travel while Europe was in the grip of war? The French and British would certainly not afford travel facilities to a revolutionary who was working for the defeat of their Russian ally. For the very same reason, however, it was in the German interest to assist Lenin. Since the beginning of 1915 the German Government had been sending large sums of money through secret channels to the Russian revolutionary movement—it is, after all, a perfectly normal way of waging war to attack the enemy inside his country as well as from outside. It was therefore natural for the Germans to agree that Lenin could travel across their territory to Russia in early 1917—carrying with him, they hoped, the germs of a second Russian revolution which might knock Russia out of the war once and for all.

Lenin was prepared to accept help from any quarter if it would bring nearer a revolution dominated by himself, but he tried to conceal his arrangement with the Germans knowing that the Russian public might misinterpret it. Revolutionary or not, the Russians would never have accepted as their political leader anyone whom they believed, however wrongly, to be acting as a German agent.

It was on 9 April by the western European calendar that Lenin left Zürich with over a score of other Russian revolutionaries, and passed through Germany in a special train. The party then travelled through Sweden and Finland. Though Lenin feared arrest on reaching the Russian frontier, leading Bolsheviks met him openly and briefed him on the situation

73

◄ The destruction of the Imperial emblem.
A contemporary artist's impression

Lenin's arrival at the Finland Station, April 1917.
A Soviet artist's impression

in the country while their train steamed on towards Petrograd.

Here, at the Finland Station, Lenin received a hero's welcome. A band played the *Marseillaise*, revolutionary troops presented arms, and he was given a bunch of flowers. In a special waiting-room once reserved for members of the Tsar's family, Lenin was formally welcomed by Chkheidze —a Menshevik leader and Chairman of the Petrograd Soviet—with a mournful speech stressing the need for all revolutionaries to work together in unity. In reply Lenin pointedly ignored Chkheidze and spoke directly to the assembled soldiers, sailors and workers. From the bonnet of an armoured car outside the station he harangued the excited crowd, telling them that world revolution was about to break out. He then drove, with an armed escort, to the Bolshevik headquarters in the palace of the ballerina Matilda Kshesinsky, and made a speech from the balcony. Though Lenin was not a great mob orator like Trotsky, being less emotional and flamboyant, he was no less forceful and effective in his quiet, incisive fashion.

74

It soon became clear that Lenin violently disagreed, not only with members of other Socialist parties such as Chkheidze, but also with most of his own followers. In his absence the available Bolshevik leaders in the capital had supported the Russian war effort against Germany and had tolerated the Provisional Government. Now, in the small hours of 4 April, Lenin ferociously lectured them over tea and snacks in the Kshesinsky Palace, and argued that they were completely mistaken. After a night's sleep he continued to lay down his policies in further speeches, and on 7 April the Bolshevik newspaper *Pravda* published these views, Lenin's so-called April Theses. His main points were that the Soviets should take power at once, overthrowing the Provisional Government, and try to end the war. Within a few days Lenin had won over most of the Bolsheviks with his forceful arguments and had confirmed himself as their leader.

12
May,
June and July

Though the Bolshevik party had gained many new members since the February Revolution, mere numbers held little significance for Lenin. He still believed that the best way to obtain control of the country was to command a small, disciplined band of professional revolutionaries—not to preside over a rabble of well-wishers, however numerous.

Unlike the members of other Socialist parties, the Bolsheviks were organising to seize power for themselves alone. They set up a military organisation to spread their ideas among the Petrograd garrison troops, and to train Bolshevik Red Guards—armed workers who might be expected to play an important part in due course. Lenin believed that violence was the key to political success, and once said that 'Power is not given up, it is taken by force.'

In early May, soon after Lenin's return to Russia, serious riots erupted in the streets of Petrograd when soldiers came out to protest against the Provisional Government for prosecuting the unpopular war against Germany too forcefully. The Foreign Minister and War Minister were compelled to resign, whereupon six leaders of the Soviet joined the Provisional Government as ministers. Previously there had been only one minister from the Soviet—Kerensky, the Minister of Justice.

Kerensky, who now became Minister of War, held the view that a military

77

◄ The Russian armies were weakened by mass desertion

victory might help to pull the country together and improve morale. He therefore planned to launch an offensive on the Russian western front, where there had been little fighting since February. In preparation for the attack he toured his armies in uniform, speaking to the troops to improve their fighting spirit. But though Kerensky was an effective orator who could whip up the soldiers' enthusiasm by calling on them to die for the Revolution, they tended to relapse into their former apathy as soon as he had finished speaking.

It was on 18 June and against the Austrians in Galicia that the Russians launched their new offensive. At first the attack was successful—but then German troops came in and heavily defeated the attackers. More and more Russian soldiers refused to go into action, or deserted and roamed the rear areas where they seemed a greater menace to the civilian population than to the enemy.

Meanwhile, in Petrograd, the worst riots since the February Revolution had broken out. Armed mobs—soldiers of the Petrograd garrison, sailors from Kronstadt, workers from the Putilov factory—surged through the capital on 3 and 4 July, loosing off their rifles and machine-guns. They smashed shop windows, tore down tram cables, and broke into private houses, looting, yelling and killing as they searched for the sharp-shooters whom they believed to have been sniping at them. They besieged the Tauris Palace, trying to compel the Executive Committee of the Soviet to take over the government and threatening certain unpopular figures. One demonstrator shook his fist at Victor Chernov, the Socialist Revolutionary Minister of Agriculture in the Provisional Government, shouting: 'Take power when you're offered it, you son of a bitch!' Rioters pushed Chernov into a car and might have lynched him if Trotsky had not intervened. However, Chernov and his colleagues on the Soviet Executive Committee still refused to supplant the Provisional Government, though politicians are not usually so firm in refusing power, and mobs of demonstrators are rarely so persistent in thrusting power on politicians whom they dislike.

The fury of the mob took even the Bolsheviks by surprise, and there is evidence that Lenin found himself in a quandary for once. If the rioters were as uncontrollable as they seemed, any attempt to seize the government on the crest of the disturbances was likely to collapse in chaos. On the other hand, would the soldiers, sailors and workers ever follow Lenin's party again if they were refused leadership in this hour of crisis? There were signs of such a reaction when rioting troops stood outside the Kshesinsky

Palace and booed the Bolshevik speakers who appealed for restraint.

The July riots subsided on the second day when the troops and workers decided to go home, leaving behind several hundred killed and wounded. A sharp reaction against so much pointless violence followed. The Bolsheviks were blamed for the uprising and accused of trying to seize power. But though that was certainly Lenin's ultimate goal he cannot have been plotting a *coup* on this particular occasion, for he was not even in Petrograd when the riots broke out.

The July riots marked a setback for Lenin. The suspicion that he might be a German spy gained wider currency and the Provisional Government helped to spread the rumour, now feeling sufficiently confident to move against Lenin's party. Troops loyal to the government drove the Bolsheviks out of their headquarters in the Kshesinsky Palace, and closed down their newspaper *Pravda* for a time. Leading Bolsheviks were arrested—including Trotsky, who demanded to be locked up with the others, though he was not yet formally a member of the Party. Lenin went into hiding in the country, disguising himself by shaving off his beard and wearing a wig.

On 8 July, Kerensky became Prime Minister in place of Prince Lvov, and formed a new cabinet. The likelihood of a seizure of power by the Bolsheviks had now receded, since the July riots had cost them so much popularity. The Provisional Government was therefore well placed to crush Lenin at this stage, and a more ruthless ruler than Kerensky would not have hesitated to do so. Kerensky, however, remained half-hearted in his measures against Bolshevism.

13

The Kornilov
Affair

For nearly two months after the setback of the July riots, Lenin and the Bolsheviks exercised caution and remained in the background, but the end of August saw the development of a new crisis which played into their hands and greatly increased their influence. This was the attempt by General Lavr Kornilov, the army Commander-in-Chief, to seize Petrograd and take control of the government by force.

Six months after the February Revolution, chaos and mob violence had led to a widespread feeling of weariness. Russia desperately needed a return to discipline, especially as she was still at war with powerful enemies. This had become a common, if by no means a general view, and those who held it included many who had occupied important positions under the Tsars and most army officers. It was such people who came to look to Kornilov as their leader.

Kornilov was the son of a poor Siberian Cossack. He was a professional soldier, a brave commander, and one of the least devious among Russian public figures of 1917. A small man with slanting eyes who looked like a Mongol, he used to travel about with a picturesque bodyguard of Turco-man soldiers from Central Asia, where much of his army career had been spent. He had been appointed Commander-in-Chief by Kerensky himself. The two men were agreed on the need for higher standards of public discipline, but soon quarrelled over other matters. It was partly a clash of temperament. Kornilov was a simple soldier—a man of action who considered Kerensky too talkative, while Kerensky felt that Kornilov did not understand politics. Both may have been right, and in any case neither trusted the other.

General Lavr Kornilov

Their differences came to the surface at the Moscow State Conference, a gathering organised by Kerensky and held between 12 and 15 August. His aim was to rally support behind the Provisional Government by inviting over two thousand people, drawn from all classes of society, to meet in a Moscow opera house and publicly settle their differences. There were representatives of the political right who had been prominent before February, such as property-owners, businessmen, liberal politicians, and officers who wore medals once awarded to them by the Tsar. There were also men of the left—trade unionists, ordinary soldiers and Socialist politicians. Of the Socialists, however, only the more moderate would attend, for the Bolsheviks boycotted the conference, and called out a general strike in Moscow while it was sitting.

At the conference the right-wingers supported Kornilov, and the left was for Kerensky, though he attempted to hold a balance and exhausted himself by delivering impassioned speeches. The discussions emphasised the disagreements between two sides which seemed to have only one thing in common—both were future victims of the Bolsheviks, who for the time being had succeeded in preventing them from using trams and taxis through the strike of Moscow transport workers.

A few days before the Moscow Conference, Kornilov had ordered his Third Cavalry Corps and the Wild Division, which consisted of Caucasian tribesmen, to concentrate near Velikiye Luki about two hundred miles south of Petrograd. As a move against Germany this would have been without purpose, but it put the Commander-in-Chief in a position to march against either Petrograd or Moscow. Kornilov told his Chief-of-Staff what he had in mind: 'It is time to hang the German supporters and spies headed by Lenin.' He also said that he wanted to hang every member of the Soviet, probably not distinguishing much between one kind of Socialist and another—he may even have been under the impression that all the members of the Soviet were Bolsheviks. But despite his rough soldierly language and lack of political insight, Kornilov seems to have been working for the good of Russia as he understood it, rather than simply to achieve power for himself.

Complex negotiations took place between Kornilov and Kerensky. On one occasion Kornilov posted his Turcoman warriors in an anteroom of the Winter Palace while he was talking to the Prime Minister. The bodyguard had machine-guns ready for use in case Kerensky should attempt to arrest his Commander-in-Chief.

With the two most important men in the country on such terms as these an open clash was inevitable. It began on 27 August, when Kerensky telegraphed to Kornilov instructing him to give up his command and report to Petrograd in person. Instead of obeying, however, Kornilov ordered his troops to advance and occupy the capital. The citizens of Petrograd could now imagine the ferocious Caucasian mountaineers of the Wild Division hanging Bolsheviks from every lamp-post in the capital, and without being over-scrupulous about whom they identified as a Bolshevik. For this reason, and because the bulk of the population still enthusiastically supported the cause of revolution, Kornilov's counter-revolutionary threat united representatives of widely differing political views behind Kerensky and the Provisional Government.

Among these supporters the Bolsheviks were prominent, though Lenin, who was still in hiding, was careful to define their attitude precisely—they would fight Kornilov, but without supporting Kerensky. The Bolsheviks now joined the Mensheviks and Socialist Revolutionaries with whom they had been on bad terms since July, and helped to set up a Committee for Struggle with Counter-Revolution. This body quickly recruited an armed workers' militia. Red Guards, the armed Bolshevik workers who had been partly repressed after the July riots, could now come out into the open and obtain rifles and machine-guns. Within a day or two about 25,000 worker-militiamen had joined up, with the result that the Bolsheviks now had a large organisation of armed men under their control—a weapon with which they might hope to seize power once Kornilov had been eliminated.

The defenders of Petrograd found Kornilov surprisingly easy to defeat, for though his regular troops could easily have routed any workers' militia, an armed clash was avoided. Railwaymen refused to move Kornilov's units, and telegraphists would not send their messages. At railway stations on their way towards the capital Kornilov's detachments found agitators who delivered fiery revolutionary speeches urging them to turn back. The attempted *coup* soon collapsed without bloodshed, except that disorderly soldiers and sailors in certain places took the opportunity to kill unpopular officers. Kornilov himself was arrested at Army General Headquarters in Mogilyov, knowing that his bid for power had failed utterly. He was killed in the following year in one of the first battles of the Russian Civil War.

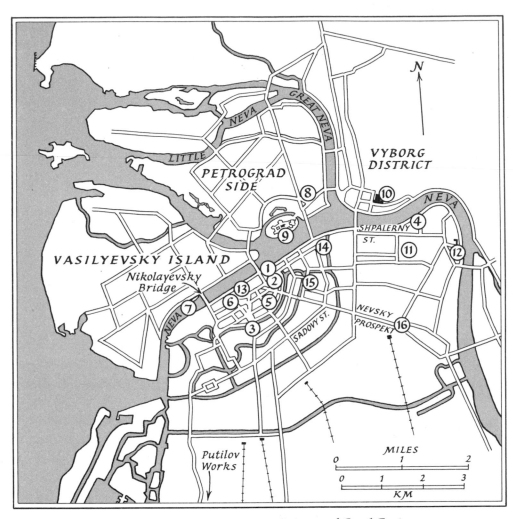

1 Winter Palace
2 Palace Square
3 Maryinsky Palace
4 Bolshevik Printing Plant
5 Telephone Exchange
6 Central Post Office
7 Location of Aurora Oct. 25
8 Kshesinsky Palace
9 Peter and Paul Fortress
10 Finland Station
11 Tauris Palace
12 Smolny Institute
13 Senate Square
14 Summer Garden
15 Site of Alexander II's assassination
16 Znamensky Square

CENTRAL PETROGRAD, 1917

14

The October Revolution

By helping to defeat Kornilov, the Bolsheviks had regained popularity, and could continue to arm and drill their Red Guards openly. The Provisional Government freed some of their leaders who had been arrested in July—among them Trotsky, who was released on 4 September. Moreover, the Bolsheviks were now obtaining, for the first time, a majority of votes in the Soviets of Petrograd, Moscow and certain provincial towns, and on 25 September Trotsky became Chairman of the Petrograd Soviet. As this illustrates, the general swing to the left was still continuing.

It appeared that Lenin's party might soon be able to take power peacefully, but this was not Lenin's own wish. Unlike most of his followers, he actually preferred to seize control by armed revolt. Though he was not in the least violent in his personal life, he seemed instinctively convinced that force would produce the best political results—perhaps because he meant to crush all opposition once he was in power, and found it logical to begin as he intended to continue. For the moment, however, he was compelled to remain in hiding, since there was still a warrant out for his arrest. In August he moved to Finland, disguised as the fireman of a train, and one of his Finnish hiding-places was the apartment of the Helsingfors Chief of Police, a Bolshevik sympathiser.

Though Lenin was still the chief Bolshevik leader, it by no means followed that other Party members were willing to obey him unquestioningly, especially as he was no longer present to harangue them in person. He continued, however, to exert great influence by writing pamphlets and articles, and by arguing with those Party members who visited his hiding places. On 7 October he secretly returned from Finland to Petrograd, once more disguised as a fireman, and hid in a private flat in the Vyborg District, a working-class suburb. Now he could once more attend meetings of the Bolshevik Central Committee, the body which determined Party policy.

Lenin considered most of his leading Party comrades too easygoing. Many of them were prepared to share power with members of other parties. Only a few wholeheartedly accepted the need for violence, and even they did not seem sufficiently aggressive to Lenin, who felt that the Bolsheviks' hour had struck. Would they ever have the same chance again if they did not seize it now? Spurred on by their leader's fierce arguments, the Central Committee took a historic decision on 10 October to seize power by force. Even then, however, no date was fixed for the rising, and no tactical plan was made.

Availability of arms and willingness to use them were of crucial import-ance, and the Bolsheviks enjoyed the advantage of being the only political group to take this problem seriously. They made every effort to obtain rifles and machine-guns for their detachments of armed workers, often by bluff or trickery. In this hunt for weapons a vital part was played by Trotsky, chief organiser of the Bolshevik drive for power while Lenin remained in hiding. One arms factory near the capital handed over five thousand rifles against an order signed by Trotsky, though he had no right whatever to make such requisitions.

Trotsky also discovered that the garrison of the Peter and Paul Fortress, on an island in the heart of Petrograd, was adopting a neutral position in the struggle between the Bolsheviks and the Provisional Government. He hurried across to the island himself and won over the troops with a revolu-tionary speech, thus putting a large weapon store in the hands of the Bolsheviks. They could now threaten to bombard the Winter Palace, seat of the Provisional Government, across the River Neva with artillery from the Fortress.

Trotsky's capture of the Peter and Paul Fortress was part of a general campaign by the Bolsheviks to obtain the support of the Petrograd garrison. As in February, the garrison troops remained of poor quality, and their

Red Guards at Bolshevik Headquarters, October 1917

morale was now lower than ever. They remained regular soldiers, however,
and could easily have defeated the Bolsheviks' armed workers in a military
engagement. Their attitude was therefore bound to play an important part
in the struggle for Petrograd in October 1917, as had already been the case
in February. Though many of these troops had little interest in political
issues, they were united in their wish to remain in the capital and avoid the
hardships of the front line. When the Provisional Government threatened,
as it did, to post garrison troops to the front, this only helped to push them
further into the Bolshevik camp.

In October the Petrograd Soviet set up a Military Revolutionary Committee which helped Trotsky to win over the garrison to the Bolsheviks.
The Committee sent its own political agents to military units in the capital,

87

replacing others appointed by the Provisional Government. It also issued an instruction that troops must not obey any military orders unless they were countersigned by a committee member.

While the Bolsheviks thus prepared themselves the Prime Minister, Kerensky, was taking part in organised public debates. His Moscow State Conference of August was followed by a Democratic Conference between 12 and 22 September, and that in turn by meetings of a so-called pre-parliament. Kerensky declared Russia a republic, and brought back the death penalty for disobedient soldiers at the front in order to help re-establish army discipline, though he did not actually impose it. He also set up on 25 September a new government, again consisting of both Socialist and non-Socialist ministers. But the Prime Minister's many efforts to bring the political right and left together only seemed to unite both sides in a dislike of himself which exceeded even their dislike of each other.

By the time Kerensky at last decided to crush the Bolsheviks by force, on the night of 23–4 October, hardly any troops in the centre of the capital remained loyal to him. He accordingly decided to bring in more reliable army units from the outskirts of Petrograd, and also to arrest the leaders of the Military Revolutionary Committee, while closing down two Bolshevik newspapers. Officer cadets—practically the only loyal force at the Provisional Government's immediate disposal—were ordered to man the drawbridge-type bridges over the River Neva and to raise them, thus cutting off the pro-Bolshevik working-class suburbs in the north from the centre of the capital. Cadets were also detached to guard such key places as railway stations and government offices, besides which instructions had been given for the cruiser *Aurora* to put to sea. She was anchored in the Neva uncomfortably near at hand, and her sailors were liable to desert to the Bolsheviks.

None of these measures succeeded. Bolshevik supporters either prevented the raising of the bridges or lowered them again. They won over the crew of the *Aurora*, and moved her to within a mile of the Winter Palace, near to Nikolayevsky Bridge, which a party of revolutionary sailors captured from the cadets who were guarding it. The Bolsheviks quickly reoccupied their printing plant, and brought out the newspapers banned by the government. On the night of 24–5 October their forces took over the telephone exchange, the central post-office and certain railway stations, meeting no serious opposition.

Thus the main effect of Kerensky's last-minute counter-measures was to

◂ Inside the Winter Palace before it fell to
the Bolsheviks on October 25–6

turn Bolshevik preparation for revolution into revolution itself.

Until the evening of 24 October, Lenin had remained in hiding in the Vyborg District on the orders of the Bolshevik Central Committee, but by this time his patience was exhausted, and he decided to make his way to the scene of action without waiting for permission any longer. He left his hideout at about 10.30 p.m. and took a tram in the direction of the Bolshevik and Soviet headquarters in the Smolny Institute, a former girls' boarding school. Since he might have been in great danger if anyone had recognised him, he wore a disreputable old cap over his wig, and had dressed like a tramp. While walking down Shpalerny Street in this disguise, he was accosted by two mounted cadets who demanded to see his papers, but he ignored them, and they rode off saying that he must be drunk. If they had insisted, the course of history might have run differently.

On 25 October, the day of the Bolshevik *coup d'état*, Lenin did not play a particularly conspicuous part, though he was present at Bolshevik headquarters in the Smolny Institute. By now Kerensky's ministers were isolated in the Winter Palace as the Bolshevik takeover proceeded. It met little serious resistance, and the restaurants, theatres, cinemas and trams continued to function. Few citizens in the capital, let alone the country at large, yet suspected that they were living through the most important political upheaval of modern times.

The only event of the day with any notable touch of drama was the storming of the Winter Palace, though even this was more of a farce than a glorious victory. By late morning the blockade of the palace by Bolshevik forces was still incomplete, and at 11.30 a.m. Kerensky was able to drive off in an official car, escorted by another car borrowed from the American Embassy. Mutinous soldiers automatically saluted him as he passed through Petrograd on his way to the front where he hoped to raise loyal forces to protect his government. Meanwhile his cabinet continued to discuss measures of defence inside the palace under the Deputy Prime Minister, Alexander Konovalov.

The Bolsheviks spent the day planning a spectacular assault on the Winter Palace, which was not well enough defended to warrant such elaborate preparations. It was decided to threaten the government with simultaneous bombardment from the cruiser *Aurora* and the Peter and Paul Fortress, but it turned out that the cannon of the fortress had been so neglected as to present more danger to the gunners who manned them than to their targets. Not until close on 7 p.m., when it had already been dark

In July 1917 Kerensky (*second from r.*) became Prime Minister. The last photograph
of him before the Bolshevik takeover in October, taken in the Winter Palace

for three hours, did the Bolsheviks send an ultimatum calling on the government to surrender.

The troops in the palace consisted only of a few Cossacks, some officer-
cadets and the Women's Battalion of Death, an unusual military unit
originally recruited by Kerensky to shame his male soldiers into fighting
more vigorously. But his government rejected the Bolshevik ultimatum,
compelled though it was to rely chiefly on women and children to defend
it in its dying hour.

Some time still had to pass before the capture of the Winter Palace, a vast
and most elaborate building originally constructed in the eighteenth
century. Through its many outside doors Cossacks of the garrison began to
desert their posts, slipping quietly away into the night while through the
same doors Bolshevik forces were quietly filtering into the building in twos
and threes. Some were disarmed by cadets in the corridors, others talked
the cadets into giving up their own arms. The Women's Battalion sallied
out to do battle, but soon surrendered.

There was an occasional crackle of fire from rifles and machine-guns.
Then, at about nine o'clock, the booming of the *Aurora*'s guns was heard
as she opened up with blank ammunition. A little later the guns of the
Peter and Paul Fortress also fired, using live rounds and breaking a few

91

windows in the palace. Meanwhile the ministers had retired from the Malachite Hall on the north side of the building to a less exposed inner room.

At about midnight Bolshevik forces rushed the palace, and began searching through the maze of its halls and galleries for the ministers. It was not until just after 2 a.m. on 26 October that the Bolshevik leader Antonov-Ovseyenko, looking more like an artist than a revolutionary in his *pince-nez* and broad-brimmed hat, intruded on them as they still sat in dignified conference. He put them under arrest. Some of his men wanted to kill them on the spot, and some started to loot the building, while others checked these hotheads by pointing out that such behaviour was un-cultured. The arrested ministers were consigned to the dungeons of the Peter and Paul Fortress, but some were freed shortly afterwards, for the more violent phase of the revolution had not yet begun, and it was unusual at this stage to murder political opponents as 'enemies of the people'.

While the Winter Palace still held out, the Second All-Russian Congress of Soviets was meeting in the Smolny Institute late in the evening of 25 October. It sat until six o'clock on the following morning. Of the 650 delegates, largely chosen by workers and members of the armed forces, about 390 were Bolsheviks, besides which the Bolsheviks also had the support of the Left Socialist Revolutionaries (the Socialist Revolutionary Party having recently split into a left and right wing). After some angry speeches, delegates of certain parties—chiefly Right Socialist Revolution-aries and Mensheviks—walked out in protest against the Bolshevik seizure of power. Trotsky jeered at them as they left, saying that they would be swept into the dustbin of history, and the congress approved a proclama-tion drafted by Lenin, in which it resolved to 'take governmental power into its own hands'.

In fact, of course, it was not the Congress of Soviets as a whole, but the Bolshevik Central Committee dominated by Lenin which now proposed to rule. However, it was a shrewd tactical move for the Bolsheviks to seize control in the name of a congress on which others besides themselves were represented, since this was likely to divert attention from the fact that a single party intended to hold power.

It was at the second session of the Congress of Soviets, on the night of 26–7 October, that Lenin at last came into his own, dominating the pro-ceedings in his shabby clothes and trousers too long for him. Now openly recognised as unchallenged leader, he received a great ovation before

Street fighting in October 1917

introducing two important decrees. One resolved to seek an immediate
peace with Germany and Austria. The other ended the private ownership
of land, establishing a national reserve of land to be made freely available
to those prepared to cultivate it with their own labour—a vague measure,
but one which had the important practical effect of appearing to confirm
the peasants in permanent possession of the estates which they had seized
from the landlords.

At the same session the Congress also confirmed the establishment of a new government, those in charge of departments being called People's Commissars, instead of ministers, to mark a break with the past. The cabinet as a whole was called the Soviet of People's Commissars, and it was as chairman of this body that Lenin became the first head of the new government. All fifteen of the first People's Commissars were Bolsheviks.

The first Soviet Government had been formed.

In other parts of the country the Bolshevik takover met with some resistance. Kerensky was still at large, and gathered a few hundred Cossack troops who captured Gatchina and Tsarskoye Selo to the south of Petrograd. But he gave up the fight on 30 October, escaped from the country disguised as a sailor, and outlived all the other main figures in the revolutionary drama of 1917 as an exile in the United States.

Moscow saw a week of heavy fighting between the Bolsheviks and those who opposed them—that is, between Reds and Whites, as the two sides had come to be called—before the city fell to the Reds.

Within a month of the October Revolution, Lenin controlled the central and northern part of the old Russian Empire, and also Siberia, its eastern part. But in the west the German armies held the large Polish and Baltic areas of the old Empire which they had overrun. The war still continued, although serious fighting had almost ceased on the Russian-German fronts. The Bolsheviks had also failed to take over the south-west and south-east of European Russia. In the south-west, part of the Ukraine refused to accept rule from Bolshevik Petrograd, and set up an independent government, the Rada, in Kiev. In the south-east, the Cossacks of the Don, the Kuban and Orenburg also asserted their independence under various local authorities.

Neither the Rada nor the Cossack régimes were firmly established. But the same could also be said of Lenin's rule in Petrograd, although there were not yet many signs that he would have to fight a bloody civil war for three years before finally achieving control over the whole country.

15

Early Bolshevik Measures

Far from restoring public order in Petrograd, the Bolshevik *coup* was followed by continuing unrest. Armed hooligans roamed the streets in the sleet of the November nights—robbing, killing and breaking into spirit stores to drink themselves berserk or unconscious. Prices soared and there was hectic gambling. Night clubs and restaurants did a thriving trade— and at the very time when famine threatened, for the food situation had further deteriorated since February.

Bolshevik prospects of holding power seemed slender. Members of their party numbered less than three hundred thousand in a country of a hundred and fifty million inhabitants. Their newly appointed People's Commissars lacked administrative experience, having previously devoted their efforts to destroying an old society, not to building a new one. Officials of the old civil service immediately went on strike against their dictatorial methods. Nor were Lenin's followers even united among themselves since his high-handed behaviour continued to antagonise more moderate colleagues, several of whom resigned from the government or Party Central Committee shortly after the takeover.

Undeterred by such setbacks, Lenin devoted his efforts to holding and strengthening the power which he had won. It was with this in view that he had so quickly brought out his two early decrees—on peace and on land

reform—calculated to increase his popularity, especially with the peasants. In seeking peasant support, Lenin also benefited from the split among the Socialist Revolutionaries—the party of the countryside—into a Left and Right wing. In November he agreed with the Left Socialist Revolutionaries that peasant delegates should join workers and soldiers on the Soviet Executive Committee. Shortly afterwards three Left Socialist Revolutionaries entered Lenin's government as People's Commissars, although they were to resign a few months later.

Lenin also tried to increase his popularity in the towns by giving workers control over their factories. He took large apartment blocks away from their private owners and handed them over to tenants' committees. If he could not feed the workers adequately, he could at least starve the *bourgeoisie* of professional people and former businessmen.

The workers had been encouraged to regard the sufferings of the *bourgeoisie* as a compensation for their own miseries, and Lenin well knew how to arouse and play on such feelings of class hatred and envy.

Besides taking these measures to make his government more popular, Lenin was determined to crush all political opposition. He began to close down newspapers which supported other parties, in effect most of the press, and arrested those who seemed hostile to his rule. He set up a special security authority, the Cheka—the 'All-Russian Extraordinary Commission for Fighting Counter-Revolution and Sabotage', to give it its full name. This was, in effect, a political police force, but the word for police was no longer used owing to its associations with the rule of the Tsars. Actually the Cheka performed the same sort of function as had the Tsarist security police, and used many of the same methods, though it was far more brutal and came to operate on a far larger scale. Cheka agents, who included criminals and drug addicts, applied a policy of 'Red terror' by seizing hostages and shooting them, and by maintaining concentration camps. Though it was directed particularly against members of the *bourgeoisie*, the Cheka terrorised all citizens, proletarians and peasants included.

The Cheka was especially helpful in Lenin's campaign to suppress all political parties except his own. He first attacked the non-Socialist parties of which the Kadets (Liberals) were the chief. Then he turned on the non-Bolshevik Socialists, and finally he attacked rebels against his authority within the Bolshevik movement itself. The process took several years to complete, since it was not at first easy for the population to re-learn obedience to authority after enjoying eight months of freedom from

97

censorship and police restraints between February and October 1917.

One important event of early Bolshevik rule was the election and dispersal of the Constituent Assembly. The Provisional Government had promised to prepare the way for such a body, which was designed to make laws providing for a permanent form of government. However, it was not until November 1917, when the Bolsheviks were already in power, that voting for the Assembly could take place. The Bolsheviks did not choose or dare to cancel this, the only free election which has ever taken place in Russia.

Having many peasant supporters, the moderate Socialists polled some sixty per cent of the votes, leaving the Bolsheviks, with only a quarter, as a minority. It was therefore widely considered that the Bolsheviks should hand over power to the Constituent Assembly. They intended nothing of the sort, however, allowing the Assembly to meet once only—on 5 January 1918, when they took care to mass troops round the meeting place in the Tauris Palace.

When the senior deputy (not a Bolshevik) tried to open the meeting, Lenin's colleague Jacob Sverdlov snatched up the hand-bell which was used to call the Assembly to order, insisted on reading a declaration of Bolshevik policy, and invited the Assembly to accept it. The other representatives refused to discuss it, and the Bolshevik members walked out. But groups of rowdy pro-Bolshevik soldiers and sailors continued to pack the galleries, interrupting the speakers with hoots and laughter, and amusing themselves by aiming their rifles at the heads of deputies.

The futile debate went on until about five o'clock in the following morning, when the Commandant of the Palace, a sailor, ordered the deputies to go home—because, he said, the palace guard was tired. On the following day the Soviet Executive Committee formally dissolved the Constituent Assembly as an organ of *bourgeois* counter-revolution, and armed guards prevented it from ever meeting again. Many of the non-Bolshevik deputies were arrested, others escaped to fight on the White side in the Civil War, and some joined the Bolsheviks.

Shortly after the dispersal of the Constituent Assembly, Russia was officially renamed the RSFSR—'Russian Soviet Federative Socialist Republic.' It was not until four years later, in 1922, that the name USSR ('Union of Soviet Socialist Republics', or 'Soviet Union') was adopted, at a conference between representatives of the RSFSR and three other republics which had since come into being—those of the Ukraine, Belo-

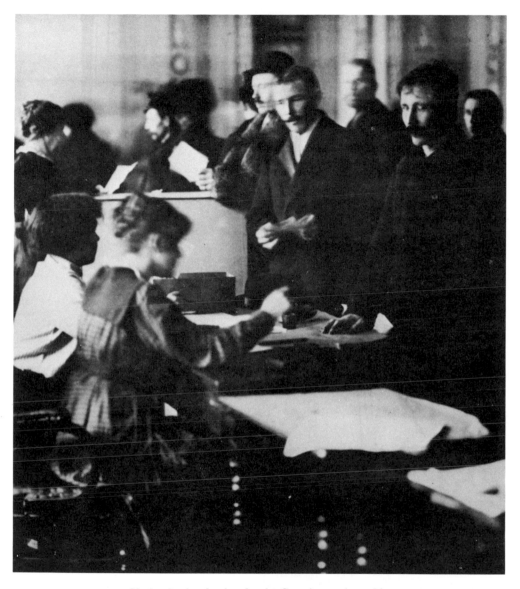

Voting in the election for the Constituent Assembly

russia and Transcaucasia. Since then the USSR has been expanded or
reorganised to include fifteen Soviet Socialist Republics in all, but the
RSFSR has continued in being as by far the largest individual republic,
corresponding roughly with the predominantly Russian-speaking areas of
the old Russian Empire, including the whole of Siberia.

16

The Peace
of Brest-Litovsk

Lenin had promised his supporters peace, and though the year 1917 had seen little action on the Russian-German front, he knew that he must keep his word since the Bolsheviks would otherwise become so unpopular that they would fall from power. Immediately after the takeover the Soviet Government accordingly began moves to arrange peace with Germany.

At the time of the October Revolution the anti-Bolshevik General Dukhonin had been in charge at Russian Army General Headquarters at Mogilyov. The government sent orders from Petrograd that he should make an armistice with the Germans and open peace negotiations. He was not willing to do so, however. Nor would he even recognise the Soviet Government, and he tried, unsuccessfully, to send his troops against Petrograd to overthrow the Bolsheviks. The Petrograd authorities accordingly ordered Dukhonin's dismissal, and sent one of their own men, Ensign Krylenko, to take over as Commander-in-Chief. Ensign was the lowest officer's grade in the army, but it was in the spirit of the Revolution that someone holding humble rank should assume command of the entire armed forces.

Krylenko reached Mogilyov on 20 November with a detachment of revolutionary sailors. They arrested Dukhonin and put him in the carriage of a train in Mogilyov station, while on the platform an angry mob of

FINLAND
INDEPENDENT 1917 (1918)

Kotlas

Vyborg
Lake
Ladoga

Helsinki

Stockholm
Kronstadt
PETROGRAD
(ST. PETERSBURG
LENINGRAD)

BALTIC SEA

Narva
Gatchina
Tsarskoye Selo
Vologda

ESTONIA
LIVONIA

Riga
Kurland

Novgorod

Pskov

Kazan

Memel
(Klaipeda)

LITHUANIA

Dvinsk

Velikiye Luki

Tver (Kalinin)

Volga

Nizhny
Novgorod (Gorky)

W. Dvina

MOSCOW

Simbirsk
(Ulyanovsk)

Gdansk

GERMANY

Vilna
(Vilnius)

Niemen

Minsk

Berezina

Mogilyov

Ryazan

Tula

Samara
(Kuybyshev)

Oka

Warsaw

Brest-Litovsk

Gomel

Oryol

Tambov

Lublin

Zhitomir

Kiev

Chernigov

Kursk

Voronezh

Vistula

Lvov

UKRAINE

Kharkov

Don

Tsaritsyn
(Stalingrad
Volgograd)

AUSTRIA

Dnieper

Poltava

HUNGARY

Jassy

Yekaterinoslav
(Dnepropetrovsk)

Lugansk
(Voroshilovgrad)

Volga

Kishinyov

Rostov-on-Don

CASPIAN SEA

RUMANIA
Bucharest

Odessa

Perekop
Isthmus

CRIMEA

Kerch

Kuban

Danube

Sofia

Sevastopol

Novorossisk

BULGARIA

BLACK SEA

Vladikavkaz
(Ordzhonikidze
Dzhaudzhikau)

Constantinople

Sukhumi

Kutaisi

Batumi

Tiflis
(Tbilisi)

Yerevan

TURKEY

Erzerum

0   100   200   300 MILES

0   500 K.M

——— Russian boundaries 1914

·—·—· Other boundaries 1914

×—×—× 'Agreed Line' (W. boundary
of Russia) by 3 Mar. 1918
Treaty

Central Powers at war with
Russia 1918

Livonia and Estonia, ceded by
Russia 27 Aug. 1918

Ukrainian People's Republic

THE PEACE SETTLEMENTS, 1918

peasants, soldiers and sailors howled for his blood. Krylenko tried to protect his prisoner, but in the end the mob tore Dukhonin out of his carriage and beat him to death.

Soon after Dukhonin's death the Soviet Government arranged an armistice with the Germans and went on to discuss peace terms in the Polish town of Brest-Litovsk. These negotiations lasted, with interruptions, from December 1917 to March 1918.

At any time during the course of the peace negotiations the Germans could have advanced and captured Petrograd or Moscow without great difficulty. The Bolsheviks, however, believed that revolution was about to engulf the whole of Europe, Germany included. They therefore expected that the German Kaiser's government would soon fall to a German form of Bolshevism, after which peace would no longer present a problem. There was, as it happened, no real prospect of a world revolution, but some of the Russians at Brest-Litovsk behaved as if there was, giving the impression that they had just won the war, not lost it. Their manner became especially domineering when Trotsky took over as head of the Bolshevik peace delegation. He shouted at the 'capitalist' generals and diplomats, flashing his eyes and gesticulating wildly as if he was addressing a Russian revolutionary mob.

Trotsky puzzled the Germans even more when, at one stage, he made the dramatic announcement that Russia would simply withdraw all her soldiers from the front—yet refuse to sign any peace treaty. He then stormed off to Petrograd in triumph, believing that he had in some way outwitted the enemy. However, General Hoffmann, representing the German High Command, simply ordered his troops to advance on a broad front. The Russians could not resist, and the result was that they were compelled to accept worse peace terms than those which the Germans had previously been willing to grant.

Lenin himself had wished to make peace earlier, and would have obtained a better bargain if the Bolshevik Central Committee had not overruled him by turning down the first German offer. Some Central Committee members supported Trotsky's unrealistic policy of 'neither war nor peace' while others were even less realistic, and urged the waging of a 'holy' revolutionary war against Germany 'with their bare hands'. But Lenin persuaded his colleagues to face the facts and make peace at any price.

By now the price was a high one. Lenin had to accept the loss of the entire Ukraine when the Ukrainian government, newly independent of Petrograd, signed a separate treaty with the Germans. He also had to surrender Poland, Finland and the Baltic countries—Lithuania, Latvia and Estonia. Though the peoples concerned were not Russians, and many of them hated Russia, their countries had all been part of the Empire of the Tsars for at least a hundred years. They represented, with the Ukraine, the results of nearly three centuries of Russian expansion.

By signing away these vast lands under the Treaty of Brest-Litovsk, Russia lost about one-third of her territory in Europe, including an important source of food in the wheat-growing Ukraine, one third of her factories, three-quarters of her coal and iron mines, and a population of over sixty millions. Uproar broke out when Lenin appeared before various Party and government bodies in Petrograd to defend his acceptance of such harsh conditions, and some delegates shouted that he was a traitor and a German spy. In the end, however, most of them voted to accept peace on his terms, having indeed no choice in the matter if they wished to retain power.

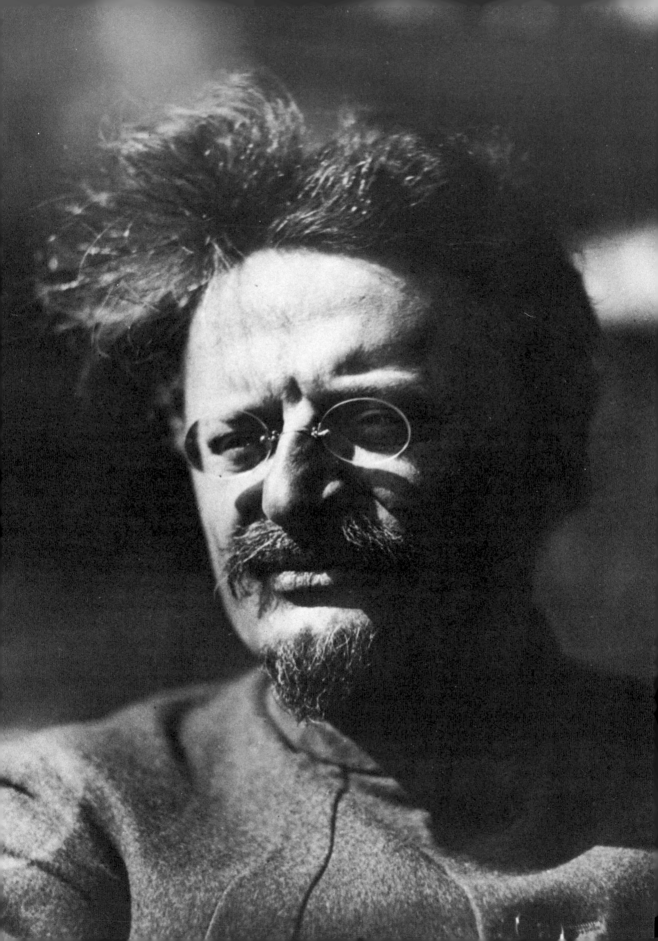

17

The Civil War: I

The Russian Civil War of 1918–20 was a struggle for the survival of Bolshevism. It was not so much a single war as a series of small wars fought on many fronts, some of them thousands of miles apart. During three years of fighting, the Reds held on tenaciously to the north and centre of European Russia including its two chief cities, Moscow and Petrograd. They were faced at one time or another by enemy armies in almost all possible directions. Though the greatest dangers developed in the east and south, there was also fighting in the far north, on the outskirts of Petrograd—and also, though not strictly as part of the Civil War, in Poland. Such, however, were the distances between the various theatres of war that the main anti-Bolshevik armies could not link up with each other, and their commanders were therefore unable to work together effectively.

Among the Whites were many who had been landowners, aristocrats, officials or officers under the Tsars, and such persons were often eager to win back their old privileges. It is noteworthy, however, that no prominent White leader ever claimed that he intended to restore the rule of the Tsars —even though White officers would sometimes sing 'God save the Tsar' in chorus when they were drunk. The White forces also contained many anti-Bolshevik left-wingers, including Mensheviks and Socialist Revolutionaries. With such violently opposed factions, conservative and radical,

105

◄ Leo Trotsky

all forming part of their camp, the Whites were weakened by continual quarrelling. Hatred of Bolshevism was the only cause which united them.

It was a war of appalling cruelty in which both sides massacred prisoners of war and civilians, while torture, mutilation and burning were everyday occurrences. Both sides were inspired by hatred and lust for revenge, for the Reds feared and hated the exploiting *bourgeoisie* and land-owners, while members of the upper and middle classes hated and feared the workers.

By no means everyone involved in the Civil War was simply a Red or a White. Individuals and units frequently changed allegiance, and brothers often fought in opposing armies. There were also many miscellaneous groups opposed to both Reds and Whites. Some consisted of Anarchists who objected to any form of government whatever, while others were bandits, using the war as an opportunity to loot under the various atamans, or chieftains, who flourished during the period. Meanwhile the vast majority of the population saw little to choose between Whites, Reds and the bandits, who sometimes called themselves Greens. Most people wanted no part at all in any of these movements, and would have preferred to be left in peace. It cannot be too strongly emphasised that the bulk of the soldiers on both sides consisted of peasants conscripted at gun point into armies which also commandeered their horses, impounded their food stores and molested their women. But there was one reason why the masses tended, on balance, to dislike the Whites even more than the Reds—the Whites threatened to restore the régime of the former landowners on estates seized by the peasantry.

Early in 1918 there was fighting between Reds and Whites in the Cossack areas of the Don and Kuban. Cossacks in general tended to be anti-Bolshevik, and the city of Rostov-on-Don, which changed hands several times, developed into a White headquarters and rallying point. Further to the west, Lenin's government sent a force to attack the new, independent Ukrainian government in Kiev, but was forced to withdraw soon after the signing of the Brest-Litovsk Treaty when the German army occupied the whole of the Ukraine.

Despite these early hostilities, no large-scale civil war seemed to loom ahead as the Bolsheviks continued to introduce various changes at home. On 1 February they adopted the western European calendar, and they also reformed the Russian alphabet. In March they changed the official name of their party to 'All-Russian Communist Party (of Bolsheviks)', and

'Shoulder to shoulder for the defence of Petrograd.'
A Bolshevik poster of the Civil War

henceforward those who have so far appeared on these pages as Bolsheviks tended more and more to call themselves Communists. Finally, and most important of all, on 11 March the capital was transferred from Petrograd to Moscow, which was less exposed to attack and which had been the old Russian capital before 1712.

A serious military threat to the Moscow government did not arise until the summer of 1918, by which time huge areas in Siberia and the east of European Russia had quickly fallen to the Whites as the result of local rebellions and sporadic fighting. This could happen so easily only because the Communist grip on the country as a whole was still extremely loose. At one stage much of the vast expanse of territory from Vladivostok in the far east to Kazan, less than five hundred miles from Moscow, was in anti-Communist hands, and it seemed that Moscow itself might fall within a matter of weeks.

This was the hope of the western Allies, who reacted to the new Russian situation by intervening in the Civil War on the side of the Whites. Though this meant deliberately meddling in Russian affairs, the Allies had several reasons for doing so. By making a separate peace with Germany, the Soviet Government had broken an agreement between Russia and the Allies, and given the Central Powers an opportunity to win the war. Bolshevik threats to provoke world revolution also antagonised the Allies, as did the confiscation of foreign property in Russia and the repudiation of Russian debts to foreigners. Above all the Allies were determined to safeguard the huge dumps of arms and other supplies which they had shipped to Russia during the war and did not wish to see in German hands.

The British, American, French and Japanese accordingly began landing troops in Vladivostok as part of a general campaign of intervention which also brought foreign troops to many other places on or near the frontiers— to Murmansk and Archangel in the far north of European Russia, to Odessa and Batum on the Black Sea, to Baku on the Caspian and to parts of Central Asia. The Allies also helped the Whites by sending them munitions and other supplies. This help was, however, limited in extent since the Allies were themselves exhausted by fighting in the west, and their peoples would not have supported any government which tried to intervene in Russia on an effective scale.

An important part in the Allied intervention was played by Czech troops, consisting largely of conscripts to the Austrian army who, after capture by Russia, had expressed a wish to go to France and fight alongside the Allies against the Austrians in order to secure Czech independence. The Russian Civil War caught most of these Czech troops in Siberia on their way to France via the Trans-Siberian Railway and Vladivostok. When Lenin's government tried to disarm them, the Czechs became anti-Bolshevik, and as the only organised military force of any importance in Siberia in the summer of 1918, they played a big part for a time in the White counter-offensive and Allied intervention against Bolshevism.

Intervention united Russians in a common dislike of foreigners, but without bringing overwhelming military forces to bear in favour of the Whites. It may therefore have benefited the Reds more than the Whites. The ineffectiveness of foreign intervention was, however, far from obvious in the summer of 1918, when Soviet Russia seemed to face disaster— threatened by Whites and foreign armies, even though admittedly small or badly organised, and without an adequate regular army of her own.

To meet this crisis Trotsky, appointed People's Commissar for War early in 1918, began to build up an entirely new force—the Red Army. He

Members of the British North Russian Expeditionary Force
in Bereznik in 1919

recruited as many Communist Party members as possible, but their numbers were insufficient, and most lacked battle and command experience. Trotsky therefore decided to conscript former officers of the Imperial Russian army. Though, generally speaking, these were opposed to Bolshevism, Trotsky forced them into the Red Army by threatening their wives and children. To discourage desertion and spying, he appointed Communist military commissars—political agents specialising in military affairs—to supervise his commanders.

This system functioned remarkably well, largely because Trotsky enforced strict military discipline. If a unit deserted in battle he was perfectly capable of having the commanding officer, commissars and one in ten of the troops shot. His headquarters was an armoured train pulled by two engines. It carried its own radio, generating plant, printing press, garage, and squad of machine-gunners. In this mobile fortress Trotsky could steam from one crisis point on the fronts to another, and wherever he went his ferocity, energy, encouragement and threats seemed to put new heart into the Red troops. To their victory in the Civil War he probably contributed more than any other man.

18

The Civil War: II

In July 1918 White forces began to threaten the Bolshevik centre at Yekaterinburg, now called Sverdlovsk, in the Urals. This happened to be where the Reds held the deposed Emperor Nicholas II, the Empress Alexandra and their children, who had all been prisoners since the abdication. When the Whites approached the town, Bolshevik guards took the Imperial Family and their servants down into a lower room and slaughtered them with revolvers and bayonets. According to Trotsky, Lenin himself ordered this mass murder since he did not want the Whites to have a rallying point in the Romanov family. The bodies were removed to a near-by mine, soaked in acid and burnt. Other members of the royal family were also murdered at about the same time.

July 1918 saw another important event in Moscow—an armed revolt against Lenin's rule by Left Socialist Revolutionaries. This was the only political party, apart from the Communist, which still functioned openly and kept representatives in the Soviets. The Left Socialist Revolutionaries disagreed with the Communists on a number of points. Amongst other things, they would have preferred the war against Germany to continue, and they now made a desperate effort to provoke a renewal of hostilities. Two men known as agents of their party tricked their way into the German embassy in Moscow. One of them shot the German ambassador, Count

◀ Victims of the Civil War, Mitava, March 1919

The Ipatyev House, Yekaterinburg (later renamed Sverdlovsk) in Siberia,
where the Imperial Family was interned and massacred

Mirbach, and threw a hand-grenade before escaping through the window.
At the same time the Left Socialist Revolutionaries tried to take power in
Moscow by a *coup d'état*. They arrested Dzerzhinsky, the head of the Cheka,
but this was one of their few positive achievements in a badly planned
attempt which the Communists easily put down—also apologising to the
Germans for the assassination of their envoy and preventing war with
Germany from breaking out again.

The Communists took reprisals against the Left Socialist Revolutionaries,
suppressed their organisation and ruled as the only legally permitted party,
though sporadic opposition by the persecuted remnants of the Mensheviks
and Socialist Revolutionaries continued for a few years. The summer of
1918 also saw the beginning of the systematic use of terror against political
opponents, and against the population at large. Hitherto torturings,
lynchings and executions by the Cheka, revolutionary soldiers and sailors
and inflamed mobs had been all too common, but had depended largely
on individual whim. Mass Red terror became official policy after 30
August, the date on which an assassin shot and killed Uritsky, head of the
Petrograd Cheka. On the same evening a Socialist Revolutionary girl shot
Lenin, wounding him twice as he returned from addressing a workers'

meeting in Moscow. As a reprisal for Uritsky's death, the Cheka executed over five hundred people in Petrograd, and the shooting of hostages among 'counter-revolutionary' groups now became a frequent occurrence. The White forces followed similar policies in the areas controlled by them.

In the summer of 1918 the Soviet Government faced an acute food crisis, since German occupation had cut off the supply of Ukrainian grain, while White operations on the Volga were also threatening communications with another main source of supply, the Kuban. In this desperate situation the authorities must somehow obtain possession of all food stocks for distribution to the starving people. There was little point in offering the peasants money in return since it was now almost worthless. Nor could manufactured commodities be offered, since industry was almost at a standstill and hardly any goods were available. The government was therefore reduced to using force, and armed squads of workers were sent from the towns to ransack the villages for food at bayonet point.

The Soviet authorities also tried to create a minor civil war in each village by setting up Committees of the Poor, the poorest peasants being encouraged to spy on the richer ones, who were called kulaks, and to search for their grain in return for a share of it. Rich or poor, Russian peasants had centuries of experience in deceiving authority, and usually did their best to hide their stocks—or distilled spirit from the grain rather than surrender it. But the forcible requisitions, combined with severe rationing which favoured manual labourers, were effective in averting large-scale famine in 1918.

The tiny official ration could be supplemented by food obtained on the black market, where the starving 'rich' would barter valuable jewellery for a few crusts of bread. This was also the age of 'sackmen'—private individuals who went into the villages and smuggled back food to the towns, hoping to evade the armed detachments which were posted at the stations to arrest such people for speculation.

By a combination of heroism, determination and brutality, the Bolsheviks weathered all the crises of 1918, and the autumn of that year saw an improvement in their military fortunes. On the middle Volga the Red Army, inspired by Trotsky, recaptured Kazan, Simbirsk and Samara, and by the end of the year many of the White gains in the east of European Russia had been wiped out. After signing an armistice with the western Allies on 11 November, the Germans withdrew from the Ukraine, and the Red Army was able to capture Kiev on 5 February 1919.

Meanwhile, however, Admiral Kolchak, a former Imperial naval officer, had become military and political dictator over the White forces in Siberia and the east of European Russia. Anti-Communist centres in other parts of the country also recognised him as their supreme military and civil authority, though their armies were too far away to make contact with his forces. In early 1919 Kolchak gained some rapid victories in his own area, his troops advancing westwards and capturing Perm and Ufa amongst other places. He had little popular support, however, some of his officers being notably cruel even by the standards of the Civil War. They murdered many of their political opponents, and also followed the usual practice of robbing peasants and recruiting them into their army by force.

By May 1919 the Reds were striking back against Kolchak. But in the meantime another White offensive, coming from the south, had begun to rob them of territory gained in the Ukraine after the German withdrawal. In October, General Denikin, commander of the White Volunteer Army, swept northwards to reach Oryol, only 250 miles from Moscow.

In the same month another White general, Yudenich, launched a lightning attack on Petrograd, and his small army burst through to the outskirts of the city.

Though these threats made October 1919 the most dangerous month of the whole Civil War for the Communists, they proved equal to the crisis.

Always eager to meet disaster head on, Trotsky rushed to Petrograd to organise its defences, after which Yudenich's small army was compelled to fall back to Estonia. Denikin was also in trouble, having over-extended his forces by advancing on Oryol while his rear and communications were under attack from the various bandit groups and private armies which infested the Ukraine. The most celebrated of these local leaders was Nestor Makhno, a young Anarchist peasant and a genius of guerrilla warfare who sided now with the Reds and now with the Whites, scouring the Ukrainian country-side with his marauding peasants who rode carts mounted with machine-guns. When threatened by superior force they would hide their weapons and melt into the landscape as peaceful ploughmen.

On 20 October 1919, Red forces drove Denikin out of Oryol, and he began to fall back southwards through the Ukraine. In March 1920 he took his troops to the Crimea. Having now lost the confidence of his officers and men, he resigned in favour of another White general, Baron Wrangel, and left the country.

Far away in western Siberia, the Whites had now lost Omsk, for some time their capital city. The defeated Admiral Kolchak was betrayed to the Reds near Irkutsk. They interrogated him, shot him without trial and pushed his body under the ice of a local river in February 1920.

Two more campaigns remained to be fought. The first of these was against the Poles, who were now a newly independent nation under Marshal Pilsudski. Feeling that this was the moment to extend their frontiers in the east at Russia's expense, they suddenly attacked, taking Kiev on 6 May 1920. But Red counter-attacks flung them back on Warsaw—after which they counter-attacked in turn, defeating the Red forces. By now Russians and Poles were weary of fighting, and they signed peace in October 1920.

Bolshevik prisoners of Admiral Kolchak's forces

Baron Wrangel

While engaging the Poles, the Red Army was also forced to fight Baron Wrangel, who skilfully reorganised the remains of the White army and burst out of the Crimea in June 1920. He gained some victories in the southern Ukraine before the Reds drove him back on his base in the Crimea. They stormed the Perekop Isthmus on the third anniversary of the October Revolution, and compelled Wrangel to evacuate his forces through the Crimean ports in late 1920. About 140,000 Whites, including the troops' wives and families and other civilian refugees, sailed off to become *émigrés* in foreign countries.

Other outlying areas of the former Russian Empire—Transcaucasia and Central Asia—were also brought under Soviet control. Finally, in 1922, Moscow gained possession of the whole of the Russian Far East when Japan withdrew her force from Vladivostok.

The victory of the Reds in the Civil War was due to their central position, to a general hatred of the old régime and of foreign interventionists, as also to better generalship, and to more determined political leadership. Above all, Communist Party members felt that they had something positive to fight for in the new society which they hoped to create, and though they formed only a minority on the Red side, their political faith was an important factor in stiffening morale and organisation. The Whites, by contrast, only had something to fight against—Bolshevik rule.

19

From 1921 to the Death of Lenin

By early 1921 the Reds had won the Civil War, and Lenin was firmly established at the head of the only Communist government in the world. However, world revolution, on which he had so long counted to rescue Russian Communism, no longer seemed a likely prospect, despite attempts to promote it through the Comintern—an international organisation of Communist parties founded in 1919 and under the control of Moscow.

When the Civil War ended, Soviet Russia was in a desperate condition. She had endured six years of fighting, losing tens of millions of citizens by battle, famine and epidemics. Her industry lay in ruins, and the production of such commodities as coal, iron and oil was down to a fraction of their level in 1914. Food and fuel were in critically short supply, and transport was badly disrupted—the railways in particular. Locomotives and rolling stock had broken down to a calamitous extent, and so crowded were the few available trains that passengers clung like flies to the sides and roofs at risk to life and limb. Townspeople had fled in large numbers to the villages, where they found their situation almost equally difficult, and Petrograd was reduced to less than a third of its former two-and-a-half million inhabitants—seeming more like a ghost city than a recent Imperial capital.

Somehow the country must be reconstructed. Yet barely had the Communist leaders crushed the Whites before they found themselves dealing with rebellion and dissent among their own followers. Within the leadership itself a 'workers' opposition' began to protest against dictatorial methods at the top. The workers' opposition also tried to protect the trade unions, which Lenin tended to treat more as a factory police designed to discipline his labour force than as an organisation set up by workers to defend their own interests.

The workers themselves were now demoralised and angry, especially in Petrograd. The winter of 1920–1 had been cruelly hard. Desperate for fuel to burn on their stoves, people broke up their furniture, or pulled down fences and derelict houses. Already half-starved, they found their miserable bread ration cut by a third, while armed detachments were still posted to stop those who tried to fetch food for their families from the villages.

A Moscow street market after NEP had legalised private trading

The result of such grievances was that in February 1921 strikes broke out among the workers of Petrograd, the very proletarians who had once been the main prop of Lenin's revolution. More alarming still was the outbreak early in March of armed revolt in another great revolutionary stronghold—Kronstadt, the island naval base in the Neva estuary about seventeen miles from Petrograd. The Kronstadt sailors were considered the most revolutionary Russians of all, but they had now taken up arms against the revolutionary government which they themselves had done so much to set up. Even Communist Party members in Kronstadt supported the revolt.

Lenin and Trotsky decided to crush Kronstadt by force. Their guns opened up on the island base, and the guns of rebel Kronstadt replied. But the only way to defeat the mutineers quickly was to make a direct assault over the ice—and it was necessary to act at once, for spring was on the way and the frozen estuary was already about to melt. General Tukhachevsky flung his troops, camouflaged in white sheets, against the island fortress and captured it on 18 March. Many rebels were executed, but many made their way to safety in Finland across the ice.

While this new revolution raged in Kronstadt, the Tenth Congress of the Communist Party was meeting in Moscow. It became one of the most important congresses in the history of the Party, for it was now that Lenin laid down two important new policies which remained in force after his death.

Firstly, he introduced a different principle of administering industry and agriculture—the New Economic Policy (NEP). It replaced the preceding economic system, known as War Communism, under which the Government had nationalised all industry, banning private trade, and trying to organise the whole of production and distribution through an army of officials.

Trotsky had wished to maintain the methods of War Communism in peace time. He had begun converting his soldiers into armies of militarised labourers and setting them to work in factories, but this produced poor results and aroused violent opposition. It was, therefore, in an opposite direction to that desired by Trotsky that Lenin decided to move with NEP by returning to a modified form of capitalism. This meant, for instance, allowing the peasants to sell their produce for what it would fetch instead of forcing them to surrender it to armed requisitioners. It now became possible to engage in private trade again and to run a private business for profit.

Lenin and Stalin shortly before Lenin's death

Though this shocked many dedicated Communists, Lenin considered it to be the only way out of chaos, intending it as a purely temporary measure —a tactical retreat in certain areas of the economy, but a retreat which still left the State in control of the larger industrial concerns.

NEP contributed to the recovery of the economy and helped to create a more relaxed atmosphere, but the other new policy laid down by Lenin at the Tenth Party Congress of March 1921 was a step in the opposite direction—a ban on all opposition by groups within the Communist Party itself to the official line as laid down from time to time by the Central Committee, and in effect by himself. Having so effectively combined to deprive all other parties of power, rank and file Communists now found themselves rendered powerless in their turn. More and more the structure of the Communist Party was resembling a pyramid, with a single figure— Lenin—as sole dictator at the top.

The year 1921 saw two further serious crises. A huge peasant revolt flared up in the province of Tambov to the south-east of Moscow, and lasted until autumn, when the Red Army under Tukhachevsky finally suppressed it. At the same time a terrible famine was raging in the Volga basin and elsewhere. It caused an unknown number of deaths—so many that the Soviet Government grudgingly permitted the Hoover American Relief Administration to distribute food to the starving. The next year's harvest was better, and the food situation began to improve.

By this time Lenin had become far more of an autocrat than most of the Tsars had been, and was also beginning to move beyond autocracy to totalitarianism—that is, to a state in which the government decides what people shall think as well as what they shall do. However, Lenin was not himself able to develop totalitarian power to any great extent, for he had hardly begun to establish it when he fell seriously ill. From December 1922 onwards he suffered a series of strokes which paralysed him and progressively deprived him of the capacity to write and take effective decisions.

Lenin was still the head of the government in name, but other leading Communists were already jockeying for position, each hoping to take power when their leader died. Though Trotsky was by far the most celebrated leader after Lenin, he had little aptitude for the necessary intrigue, or thought it beneath his dignity. Meanwhile a less conspicuous figure— Joseph Stalin, whom many of his colleagues considered a complete nonentity—was patiently organising support for himself behind the scenes.

Stalin, a Georgian who had been educated at the theological seminary in Tiflis, was not a theorist or intellectual. But his immense patience, and unusual capacity for intrigue and treachery, enabled him to outwit rivals who seemed, superficially, far cleverer than he. Stalin's crude methods alarmed Lenin, as he stated in a political testament written during his last years. He was unable, however, to check Stalin's rise towards supreme power from his sickbed, and the testament was officially suppressed for many years after his death.

Lenin died on 21 January 1924. His body lay in state in the Hall of Columns in Moscow, and many thousands queued in the freezing cold to file past it, after which it was embalmed and put on display in the mausoleum on the Red Square. In his honour the authorities changed the name of their second city from Petrograd to Leningrad—part of an elaborate cult of Lenin by his successors, who began to refer to him as a god in the hope of conferring additional importance on themselves as his high priests. Lenin, who disliked ostentation, would never have allowed such a cult to develop in his lifetime.

122

20

After
Lenin's Death

Within a few years of Lenin's death the struggle for power among the Soviet leaders ended in a decisive victory for Stalin. By 1928 he had emerged as unchallenged dictator, more feared than Lenin but less popular. He maintained his supreme position for a quarter of a century until his death in 1953. Meanwhile, almost certainly on Stalin's orders, Trotsky had been assassinated in exile in Mexico City in 1940.

Stalin presided over the industrialisation of Russia based on a sequence of five year plans. He ended NEP, and replaced private farming with the enforced enrolment of peasants in collective or state farms operating as corporate enterprises. When the peasants resisted, as they did most stubbornly, Stalin had them shot or deported *en masse*, while many also perished in huge famines caused by the disruption of agriculture attendant on collectivisation. Stalin strengthened the security police, known during much of his period as the NKVD. He staged show trials of many leading Communists and officials, besides having many millions of Soviet citizens —political opponents or merely the unlucky victims of denunciation and accident—put in concentration camps. He maintained huge networks of these spread over enormous areas of the country, especially in Siberia and the far north. Russia's experiences under Stalin also included the defeat of Hitlerite Germany in the war of 1941–5.

After Stalin's death Soviet citizens lived under a government less terror-istic in its methods, but unchanged in its essential characteristics, though at least large numbers of those who had survived systematic underfeeding and overwork in the concentration camps were released.

More than half a century of Soviet rule has transformed Russia into a powerful military and industrial complex, able to hold her own with the United States in the competition to explore space and threaten the destruc-tion of the world. It is in establishing military power and creating a massive industrial base that Soviet Russia has attained her most outstanding successes—not in creating individual prosperity for the average citizen. As for the right to read, speak, think, associate and travel according to individual desire, conditions became less severe after Stalin's death, but without conferring anything which remotely approaches freedom as it is taken for granted in non-totalitarian societies.

Overthrowing an authoritarian régime, the Russian revolutions of 1917 have thus led to the creation of a system different in many ways—not least in being far more authoritarian.

Meanwhile other countries, including China, have also adopted Com-munism, while sometimes disagreeing violently with Moscow on how a Communist society is to be organised. But the general upheaval predicted by Lenin has not taken place, though official spokesmen of the Soviet Union persist in maintaining that their revolution is only a prelude to world revolution. They also imply that it represents the greatest and most beneficial change which has ever taken place in human society.

Though Marxists believe that the Russian revolutions of 1917 were brought about by the working of inexorable historical laws, it can also be argued that the accident of human personality played a certain part. Would the Russian monarchy necessarily have fallen in February without the combined weakness and obstinacy of a Nicholas II to help push it over the abyss? Could a single party have established a totalitarian dictatorship without the drive, single-mindedness and political genius of a Lenin to capture power in October and consolidate it during the next few years?

124

BOOKS FOR FURTHER READING

CHAMBERLIN, William Henry, *The Russian Revolution, 1917–1921*, 2 vols. (New York, 1935)

FLORINSKY, Michael T., *The End of the Russian Empire* (New York, 1961)

—— *Russia: a History and an Interpretation*, 2 vols. (New York, 1947)

GREY, Ian, *The First Fifty Years: Soviet Russia, 1917–1967* (London, 1967)

HINGLEY, Ronald, *Nihilists: Russian Radicals and Revolutionaries in the Reign of Alexander II, 1855–1881* (London, 1967)

——*The Tsars: Russian Autocrats, 1533–1917* (London, 1968)

KATKOV, George, *Russia in 1917: the February Revolution* (London, 1967)

RAUCH, Georg von, *A History of Soviet Russia* (London, 1957)

SETON-WATSON, Hugh, *The Decline of Imperial Russia, 1855–1914* (London, 1952)

—— *The Russian Empire, 1801–1917* (Oxford, 1967)

SHUKMAN, Harold, *Lenin and the Russian Revolution* (London, 1966)

ULAM, Adam B., *Lenin and the Bolsheviks: the Intellectual and Political History of the Triumph of Communism in Russia* (London, 1965)

WOLFE, Bertram D., *Three Who Made a Revolution: A Biographical History* (London, 1956)

INDEX